D1234885

A Time to Kill, a Time to Heal

An Israeli Navy SEAL's Journey

YOTAM DAGAN

gefen
publishing house
JERUSALEM • NEW YORK
Est. 1981

Scripture quotations are modified from *The Holy Scriptures According to the Masoretic Text*, published by the Jewish Publication Society in 1917.

Cover design: Jaki Levy
Cover illustration: Jaki Levy
Typesetting: Optume Technologies

ISBN: 978-965-7023-47-1

1 3 5 7 9 8 6 4 2

Gefen Publishing House Ltd.
6 Hatzvi Street
Jerusalem 9438614,
Israel
972-2-538-0247
orders@gefenpublishing.com

Gefen Books
c/o Baker & Taylor Publisher Services
30 Amberwood Parkway
Ashland, Ohio 44805
516-593-1234
orders@gefenpublishing.com

www.gefenpublishing.com

Printed in Israel
Library of Congress Control Number: 2020916685

To everything there is a season,
and a time to every purpose under the heaven:
a time to be born, and a time to die;
a time to plant, and a time to pluck up that which is planted;
a time to kill, and a time to heal;
a time to break down, and a time to build up...

Ecclesiastes 3:1–3

And a time to love.
This book is dedicated to Iris,
my partner in this life's journey,
who believed in me and was willing to wait.

Contents

Part Four: A Time to Heal

Foreword

This story is about the reflection of the light and infinity of the human spirit. It is about post-traumatic growth. About cold, dark places underwater and the bright light above. The power of positive human relationships. For everything and everyone, there is a season. This life story by Yotam Dagan of the growth and development of a young warrior into a sage healer is universal in time and place.

It is a remarkable, unusual, and probing story of an elite Navy SEAL warrior who becomes a team leader, a chief instructor, a commander, and then a psychologist. A subsequent leader in a complex crisis negotiating team and then global expert in resiliency training and PTSD prevention. A healer.

How does this happen? How did he learn?

I have been a close friend of Yotam's for ten years. We have shared a lot. We have seen the insides of each other's souls. It is with this profound honor that I write this foreword.

Yotam outlines his story with a passage from Ecclesiastes. A time to kill, a time to heal. King Solomon in Ecclesiastes redirects the wisdom of the principle of retributive justice, attributing a time for all seasons.

Yotam's story is one of service, pain, suffering, and growth, and then more, and even more growth. It is an optimistic story. It is Ecclesiastes and Sir Thomas More's devotion to his conscience, engaging, to become a human for all seasons. Renaissance humanism in its broadest sense.

The elite Shayetet 13 Navy SEAL unit is shrouded in myth and mystery. There are many stories Yotam cannot tell. What he does tell he humanizes, and then he tells us about emotions and vulnerability. Moreover, we learn that in addition to all usual measures of high performance, a significant "secret sauce" in the glue that holds these super teams together is relationships and emotions. Even more, it is the trust of compassion and empathy. Indeed, we learn, it is the same for all of us. Deep relationship support (empathy) is the one constant that enables resiliency, adaptability, and functional continuity. *Trust.*

It is empowering to read and understand how Dagan cultivated emotional honesty and the resilience that springs from it in elite special forces soldiers and then applied these tools to multiple civilian populations, all over the world, for healing. That peer-to-peer support of empathy and compassion enables profound resilience and adaptability. *Flexibility.*

I think there is meaning for all of us in these pages. This is a story of the human spirit, of its massive ability to reflect infinite light. *Perseverance. Resilience.*

Beyond passing BUD/S training, becoming a leader, and serving, this is about being a human for all seasons. Moreover, Dagan touches on the crucial willingness to be vulnerable, in order to be strong. Connecting with another fellow human being in order to share, listen, and show empathy. And then, the remarkable human and organizational growth in power and healing that comes out of this.

Dagan addresses the opportunity embedded in a crisis situation. Indeed, as the world spins on COVID-19, there is wisdom and experience here that could be helpful to us. If we can connect with each other in the ways Dagan describes (willing to be vulnerable to be strong, listening with empathy) and cultivate as he does a resilient and flexible network, we can continue to move toward an optimistic future.

A time to heal.

Jonathan Lewis, MD, PhD

Closing Circles of Destiny

Looking ahead into the dark, I could see the sparkling lights of plankton, tiny marine creatures illuminating the water. Underwater, my compass, depth gauge, and diving watch confirmed that we were headed in the right direction. Staff Sergeant Ran, my diving buddy and good friend, was a little behind me, to my right. We were heading toward our target in enemy waters. The mission was clear: to eliminate ships at anchor in an enemy port. Our intelligence indicated that they were to serve as mother ships to carry out an attack against civilians in Israel. Onboard the ships were Zodiac rubber boats, AK-47 Kalashnikov assault rifles, RPG anti-tank rockets, and plenty of ammunition. The Palestinian terrorists who had been trained for their deadly mission were set to execute their attack two nights later. This was a race against time.

As a young Navy SEAL team leader, I was in command of diving pair number 2. Lieutenant Commander Shay, my commanding officer, was leading diving pair number 1. He was the commander of the two pairs of the diving force and was responsible for executing the mission.

Once underwater, with no radio communication, Ran and I were on our own. At a depth of fifteen feet, sensing the cool water around me, I shivered and became aware of my increased heartbeat. My senses were heightened, and I was highly alert. This was the real thing, not another exercise.

Swimming fast, closing the distance to the enemy targets, stealthily making our way toward the harbor, I had a moment to contemplate the significance of this operation. The objective of this operation was to thwart a deadly terrorist attack on Israeli civilians. In my mind's eye, I could see the terrorists who had arrived in Zodiac rubber boats and attacked my kibbutz eleven years earlier. I felt the same shivers that I had felt then as I was hiding in the brush.

I recalled the attack that almost cost me my life and definitely changed it forever. Now we had to stop them.

As we snuck into the well-guarded compound from the deep Mediterranean into the shallow, illuminated water of the inner port, it became more difficult to move unnoticed. Following the plan, I managed to navigate to the designated location inside the harbor. I needed to surface briefly to identify my target, note the right direction on my compass, and then continue. I would be exposed for three to four seconds and would be vulnerable if seen. It was supposed to be in a safe place, hidden from the pier. But it wasn't.

As I approached, moving my fins slowly, I realized that the water was too shallow to continue toward the planned location. The pier was well lit, and I knew that armed patrols would be scanning the area. Suddenly the lights went out, probably due to a power outage. I took a quick peek just above the water. Looking in the direction of my target, I identified "my" ship, my target. In the other direction, I spotted an armed patrol about five yards away: two terrorists and a dog. At that moment, the lights went back on. Diving immediately, I grabbed Ran, pushing him slowly toward the sandy bottom, away from the pier toward deeper water. I knew that if they saw me, they would shoot their AK-47s, which didn't worry me too much because I knew that bullets lose velocity when they hit the water. What did worry me was that they probably had hand grenades as well, a real threat for divers. A grenade explosion near our position would most likely kill us both.

I had no time to explain. Nor did I have time to check my compass to decide in which direction we needed to go. It was too risky. So I decided to continue according to the preplanned course we had calculated back on base. The water got deeper as we dove away from the pier and crossed the route that the boats use to enter and exit the harbor. I was supposed to make sure that no fishing boat would run us over in the shallow water, but circumstances wouldn't permit that. When you're blind, you use your other senses to guide you. I listened intently but heard only the hum of distant motors.

As we crossed the entrance route, I tried to collect my thoughts and feelings. I wasn't sure I had done the right thing, and I hoped for the best. My diving buddy had no idea where we were and was dependent on me, as I was the navigator as well as the leader of our pair. Alone underwater, I felt the responsibility weighing heavily on my shoulders. The sandy bottom became muddier as the water became shallower. It was hard to move without risk of discovery. "Am I in the right place?" I asked myself. I stopped and looked up, my diving mask just an inch below the surface, surveying my surroundings, seeing as if through a panoramic lens. I saw a small white ship just to my left. I swam forward and under it and turned to the bow to identify it. The boat's name was clearly written there. It was our target.

Feeling a great sense of relief, I had no time to celebrate. Using hand signals, I conveyed our next steps to Ran: set the limpet mines (explosive devices with preset time detonators) and activate them. We completed our task and set out on the long dive to exit the harbor, where we were to be picked up by our SEAL delivery boats.

Once outside the harbor, we dove to a safe distance and then surfaced slowly. I looked around and gave Ran the all-clear. We removed the diving mouthpiece, breathing in fresh air, smiling with relief as we inflated our buoyancy control devices. A few minutes later, we were back on our boat. Our sense of accomplishment was huge while we anxiously awaited the other diving pair, who had maintained complete radio silence for several hours. Half an hour later, having fulfilled their mission as well, diving pair 1 boarded the boat, and we started out on the long way home.

When the target boats exploded, we had the satisfaction of knowing that a deadly terrorist attack had been thwarted.

PART ONE
BEGINNINGS

Go out there, be tough, fight wars, and live to write about it. Contract your stomach muscles when you need to shoot, read poetry, and shed a tear. When I look back and contemplate my childhood, it seems to have had some elements of a modern Sparta.

CHAPTER 1

The Spartan Days

Kibbutz Life

Decades before it came to be known as the "start-up nation," with its spark of innovation and cutting-edge technology, Israel in the 1960s and 1970s was a young and vibrant land. Israelis perceived their existence according to the security situation at any given time. The national mood was determined by the events leading up to wars or by their outcome.

The 1967 Six-Day War was a huge military victory, boosting Israel's sense of power and invincibility. In just six days, the Israel Defense Forces (IDF) captured the Egyptian Sinai Peninsula, the Jordanian-held West Bank of the Jordan River, and the Syrian Golan Heights, leaving the Syrian, Egyptian, and Jordanian armies defeated. This sense of euphoria proved to be short-lived.

The 1973 Yom Kippur War, in which Israel was caught unprepared, had a chilling effect on the Israeli collective psyche. Israel paid a heavy price in casualties, and the public lost confidence and trust in its political and military leadership. The national mood seemed to resemble the emotional turmoil of a teenager. On this roller-coaster ride of emotions and public opinion, the young Israeli society began its maturation process. It was an era characterized by a sense of Zionist renewal. There was an existential urgency in the wake of the Yom Kippur War, while at the same time, there was a yearning to live normal lives, to earn a living and to feel secure. In other words, we wanted to be a nation like all nations.

This was the context in which I came to be. This was the narrative of the day, the setting, and the background music.

I was born in 1966 on Kibbutz Maagan Michael, a small communal village on Israel's Mediterranean coast. I remember the hillside with a few small houses on it. I can still feel the cool floor and smell the unique scent of the cleaning fluids used in the children's house.

Even today when I walk barefoot in the warm white sands of the kibbutz beach, I relive childhood memories. Looking eastward toward Mount Carmel, I see the familiar limestone cliffs illuminated by the last rays of the sun setting into the sea.

I am part of the third generation of Israeli nation builders. My grandparents on both sides were brave, determined pioneers who were also intellectuals seeking broader horizons, feeling fortunate to have escaped Europe before the Holocaust. Only later did I realize that their Zionist ethos ran in my veins and is at the core of my identity. During my childhood years, this ethos evolved into that of the modern Israeli warrior: an unlikely yet appealing mixture of the sword and the plowshare, of Herman Melville's *Moby Dick* and the cynicism of Joseph Heller's *Catch-22*. Go out there, be tough, fight wars, and live to write about it. Contract your stomach muscles when you need to shoot, read poetry, and shed a tear.

When I look back and contemplate my childhood, it seems to have had some elements of a modern Sparta. Since its foundation in the late 1940s and well into the '80s, my kibbutz epitomized an ideological setting with a strong sense of purpose. The kibbutz movement took a central role in the foundation and the defense of the young State of Israel. In what was perhaps one of the most unusual social experiments of the twentieth century, the kibbutz strived to be a utopian society. Kibbutz economics were based on the Marxist equation "From each according to his ability, to each according to his needs," and there was a noticeable lack of correlation between work and compensation.

The experimental communal child-rearing practices were extremely innovative. As in many experiments, the outcome of communal child-rearing would only be felt and studied in the years to come. Growing up on a kibbutz was definitely a challenge to one's emotional development and well-being. Aspiring to live a productive life of work and contributing to the kibbutz, parents were relatively hands-off where the children were concerned. Children were raised separately, in children's houses, a sort of dormitory/boarding school arrangement in which trained caregivers looked after us, almost from birth.

In the children's house where I lived, I learned my first lesson in coping. One of my earliest childhood memories, at the age of two or three, was waking in the middle of the night, everyone asleep around me, with sharp pain. I had an ear infection – foreshadowing my future as a Navy SEAL diver (divers tend to suffer recurrent ear inflammations, due to the exposure to water and to the pure oxygen used in military diving gear). The pain was terrible. I can still see the window high above my crib, stars shining in the cloudless sky. I can hear the calm breathing of the other three children sleeping in the adjacent cribs in our room. There was no caregiver or responsible adult in the children's house. My parents were probably sleeping in their room about two hundred yards away. It didn't even occur to me that they should be there for me. It was not part of the deal.

In the children's house, all of the physical needs were met, but not enough thought was given to our emotional needs. I was on my own. There was no other option. Much later I reflected: the fact that there was no one to turn to along with the yet unverbalized notion that I had to cope alone in times of need resulted in a crippling sense of emotional detachment as I grew up. The ability to cope by myself became my method for survival as the tough loner. Contract your stomach muscles and be strong. Don't cry or ask for help, because no one will be there to offer help or support.

It took me years to recognize this trait in myself and a lot of hard work to modify this pattern of behavior. I had to learn that it was legitimate to be needy at times and that to be dependent on others was not a flaw. I felt success when, as an adult, I learned to allow myself to be touched and cared for as might be done for a small child.

The upside of communal living was the daily leisure time spent with the parents. From four o'clock in the afternoon until seven in the evening (and longer on the weekends), quality family time was usually about having fun. Housekeeping chores were almost nonexistent, as meals were prepared and served in a communal dining room, laundry was washed centrally, and kids were taken care of for most of the day and night.

We were fortunate that the kibbutz was located only five hundred yards from the Mediterranean coast, so we spent a lot of our free time at the beach, snorkeling and bodysurfing in the warm summer sea water, swimming to a small group of rocky islands that rose out of the sea about two hundred yards from the beach. We would occasionally use a flashlight and look for shore crabs at night – watching them in the hundreds, roaming the beach. We collected seashells or just played in the sand, building sand castles or playing soccer. The kibbutz was considered a safe zone, in which children could roam freely and play. We used to explore the cotton fields, the dairy farm, the fishponds. Happy and carefree, we grew up as if in a dream.

In middle school, we started our nautical training. We learned how to row a boat, maneuvering with the use of the oars, raising anchor, and setting sail. It was an active childhood, filled with cool things – an enriched education. It should have been the utopian way to raise children. For some, including for me during my teenage years, it seemed to be. For many others, including myself using hindsight many years later, it turned out to be much more complicated.

Emotional Detachment

External events during childhood impact personal and emotional development, and in many ways shape one's character. In retrospect, it is puzzling to see the extent to which my personal development as a six-year-old boy could become enmeshed in the enormous events that were about to transpire.

Yom Kippur 1973 was one of those days ingrained in the Israeli collective memory. It was just before my seventh birthday, and, of course, I was too young to understand the meaning and implications of the terrible war that would break out that day.

My grandparents were part of the Zionist movement in Europe before the Second World War. They grew up in traditional, middle-class Jewish homes. When they arrived in their ancient (but new) homeland, they distanced themselves from most of the traditional and religious aspects of Judaism. They exchanged the old world and the traditions of the Jewish Diaspora for a life devoted to modern agriculture and the socially based neo-Jewish kibbutz life. What this meant to us modern-day kibbutzniks was that there would be no visit to the synagogue that Yom Kippur morning. Instead, my parents took my younger brother and me to the beach.

With the warm Israeli October sun in the sky above and the silky white sand beneath our feet, we joined many others for a day of fun at the beach. The clouds traveled swiftly across the skies, reflecting off the grayish-blue Mediterranean waters. It was deceptively beautiful and dramatic; there was no hint of the existential military storm approaching. The autumn wind blew, and the sea grew rough, the waves growing higher and higher, perhaps in warning of what we did not see.

Standing in the waist-high water, my father held me in his arms, raising me up above each breaking wave. I was happy and felt fearless. My father held me, smiling and laughing, high above the waves. Suddenly a huge wave, a wave too big for my dad to hold me aloft, rushed toward us. With no time to explain, my father did the only reasonable thing he could do. He held me tightly in his arms and dove headfirst into the rising wave. Surprised, eyes and mouth wide open, I swallowed water and felt the sting of the saltwater in my eyes. When the wave passed and I regained my breath, I was outraged. I felt betrayed. Crying, I ran out of the water to the shore. I did not look back but walked barefoot along the long hot path, all the way to the children's house. It was probably the first time I felt real anger toward my father.

I waited for him to come to me. I needed to be hugged and comforted. He didn't come. I did not know that the war had broken out and that my father, a captain in the infantry reserves, had been called up and had joined his unit. He led his men in the fight against the Syrian army in the Golan Heights and came home only about three or four months later. Those trying days turned into weeks of anticipation and fear. Nights were shattered by air-raid sirens. At their wail, we would run to the bomb shelters, trying to comprehend what was going on. I remember seeing my mother sitting on the grass with other kibbutzniks, whispering while they listened to a portable transistor radio. Bad news kept coming in from the battlefields; the names of wounded and fallen soldiers and those missing in action were shared, delivered by IDF officers who came to the kibbutz. These officers then had to continue on their impossible mission delivering their terrible news in the next locale.

This surreal situation lasted for a long, long time, an eternity for a child who understood little of this dire situation. I waited for my father to return, to appease me. When you're seven years old and express your anger so clearly, and the object of your anger disappears, the lesson is there to be learned. It seemed to reinforce my feeling of emotional detachment and the absolute necessity to be self-sufficient.

Diving Deep in Search of Lost Emotions

I started diving at a very young age – that is, if you can count an involuntary dive as a diving experience. One of my earliest memories was of such a dive. I was two or three years old, and I was spending Saturday morning at the beach with my father and our new rubber mattress. The water was warm, the sea calm and inviting. I didn't yet know how to swim but felt secure with my dad at my side. A small wave caught my father unaware, upsetting the mattress, and I rolled off into the water. Surprised to find myself underwater, I felt the warm embrace of the sea as I sank deeper and deeper, eyes wide open. I vividly recall the sensation of sinking and the feeling of pressure building in my ears. I was too young to imagine that I might be drowning, and my memory of the experience conjures up a feeling of tranquility. When my father dove in after me and brought me back up to the surface, I gulped the fresh air but I didn't cry. The feeling of being weightless in a noiseless environment had left its mark on me and become embedded in my personality. It set the tone for who I have become: a diver exploring the emotional sphere. I listen carefully and connect, try to heal others, and seek a meaningful existence.

Many years later, as a young Navy SEAL, I experienced a feeling of déjà vu during one of my first dives.

It was a hot summer night, and we were about to start diving. My dive buddy and I entered the water, walking off the reef, into a long and narrow cleft that opened into the endless sea. As I donned my diving mask, adjusting the straps behind my head, and put the oxygen rebreather mouthpiece in my mouth, I sensed the sharp, cool taste of oxygen, with a touch of soda lime, a chemical that absorbs carbon dioxide. As we moved into the deeper water, I inhaled deeply to make sure that my equipment was in working order. I sweated in my rubber wetsuit, so the water was both refreshing and a bit scary at the same time. We were to swim through the cleft, between its high walls, out into the dark. Advancing from the narrow cleft into the open sea, with the seemingly infinite depth of water beneath us, was an experience of grandeur, of awe.

Carl Jung, the early twentieth-century psychoanalyst, wrote about the human race's shared or collective unconscious and about certain archetypes or themes that are part of humanity's shared identity. He described the archetypal genealogical uterus, the symbolic ocean from which life evolved and the human race was born in the evolutionary rise of life from sea to dry land. This night dive experience was like such a birth, but somehow, in the opposite direction: slowly moving from dry land through the cleft in the reef, like a birth canal, and into the warm, inviting uterine water of the sea.

For me this event symbolized my personal journey, connecting memories of previous underwater experiences with submerged layers of my own evolving identity. In the deep waters of the Mediterranean Sea, I experienced rebirth, growth, and a connection with my deepest, subconscious emotions.

Parents, Children, Community

The kibbutz developed as an idea and became a way of life during the twentieth century. The first kibbutz, established in 1909, was Degania. These early pioneers were considered the poster children of the Zionist revolution. These young men and women worked hard and enjoyed a meaningful life, creating a unique social structure. Tanned, strong, and determined, they were innovative in many aspects of their communal lives. They invented machines for agriculture; they wrote their own interpretations for celebrating the Jewish holidays; they created new traditions and rite of passage rituals that we, generations later, still follow.

They would gather weekly in the large dining hall, the heart of the community, and engage in long, often heated discussions regarding all aspects of their communal life. This unique energy fed an ecosystem that inspired growth and development. Some members were sent to study and became engineers, returning to the kibbutz and creating thriving industries; others became political and military leaders. There was, however, a consensus as to what kibbutz life should look like. All of these pioneers were expected to abide by the decisions made by the collective during these weekly gatherings, which were voted upon by a show of hands. Those who could not adhere to these decisions left the collective. The ones who remained became members of the kibbutz. Both of my parents were born on a kibbutz, my mother on Maagan Michael and my father on Kibbutz Afikim, in the Jordan Valley. They were the offshoots, born to these ideas and this way of life. The kibbutz ideology was totally ingrained in them, and they were committed to its success.

As children of the kibbutz, we became part of the pack – the peer group – living, eating, playing, and sleeping together. There is no doubt that this communal upbringing would become the defining factor in our personal development. From birth to early care, from kindergarten throughout our school years, the same group evolved and was shaped by this unique child-rearing practice. Not that we became carbon copies, but our personalities developed and were influenced deeply by this communal experience. To this day, I think of this group of individuals as my alter-siblings. A group of fifteen children, sharing dormitories, show-ers, meals, playtime, and school. We spent more than twenty hours a day together, and although there was often friction and fighting, we knew each other intimately. Lifelong bonds were made. There was a strong sense of pride and belonging to the kibbutz.

About a hundred feet away from my children's house was another one. It comprised another pack, three years younger than my peer group. One of the children who lived there was Idan, or Danny, as he calls himself today. As a boy, Danny was extremely smart and sensitive. In the ultra-Spartan, macho kibbutz society, he was different. Very different and special. While most of us didn't take school very seriously, while we worked out and devel-oped muscles, Danny learned Latin and Arabic. He started writing poetry and prose during high school, and in his senior year, he insisted on taking Shakespearean English as part of his matriculation exams. When his teachers said it was impossible, had never been done before, and that there wouldn't be anyone to assist him, he just showed them that he could do it, earning a perfect A. Because of his unique character, he took a lot of flak from his classmates, from my classmates, and sometimes from me. He had to cope with his intense emotions in a very detached, rough, emotionally restrained environment. Danny is my brother.

Israel's military signal intelligence unit, unit 8200, is a leading brand in Israel's "start-up nation" scene. Danny was recruited to one of its subunits and had a meaningful military service. After his discharge from the military, he paved a successful path in the evolving world of the internet, social networks, and business.

In those days, as I have described, "natural" siblings did not share enough time together to bond as brothers. We spent a mere two or three hours a day together at our parents' house and a few hours more during the weekend. The kibbutz educational setting, separating children by age group, did not promote sibling bonding. It took us many years to bridge this gap and to strengthen our relationship, as adults.

To this day, some of my children's house peers hold on to the notion that this was a perfect childhood. Others are still angry at the kibbutz system that deprived them of a "normal" family and siblinghood.

In the historical context of nation building, sacrifice, and ideology, it was a given, a necessity. It came with a huge price and emotional toll.

From the Eastern Med to the Midwest, and Back

Walter Fischgrund was born in a small town in the Czech Republic, around the turn of the twentieth century. He was a successful athlete and an excellent student. In 1936, he started to pursue his dream of becoming a veterinarian. He finished his second year summa cum laude, but after the Nazis overtook his country, he was kicked out of the university. The official reason: he was Jewish.

His sweetheart, Elza, managed to flee to London and there to bribe her way into getting emigration certificates for both of them. Just as the Second World War broke out, the couple arrived in Eretz Yisrael and settled in Kibbutz Afikim, in the Jordan Valley. They later married and changed their last name to Dagan.

Veterinary studies did not exist in Israel until the 1980s. Nation building, fighting wars to defend the young nation, and other pressing issues prevented Walter Fischgrund (who now called himself Shimon Dagan) from going back to school. Instead, he helped build a successful dairy farm and an innovative agricultural start-up that developed milking equipment. Years later, his son – my father – followed his own sweetheart and moved to Maagan Michael, where he ran the local dairy farm.

The ethos of my grandfather's vet turned dairy farmer story became an expectation. Somehow, I was expected to take that historical incident and get it fixed. I was to be the first vet in the family. As things turned out, that's not what I became. But on the way, my father took upon himself to study dairy husbandry, and since that too was not possible in Israel of the 1970s, we relocated to St. Paul, Minnesota, in the winter of 1975 for a year.

For the eight-year-old kibbutznik that I was, arriving in America was a shock. The New York skyscrapers; the deep snow that covered the Midwest, and this new culture and language were a thrilling experience. In a few weeks, I mastered basic English. In a few months, I switched to speaking only English. When I landed back in Israel, in the summer of 1976, I had nearly forgotten my Hebrew.

Being bilingual is a gift that goes way beyond the mastery of a second language. It opens up thinking, enriches concept formation, and induces mental flexibility. Landing back in Israel, reentering into the pack of children and reclaiming my former position, was not easy. I saw things differently now. I had more perspective. Leaving behind the memories of skyscrapers, the snow, and the American culture, as well as the experience of living at home, with my parents and brother, I reclaimed my Israeli kibbutznik identity. American life receded into a long-lost dream. It would take nearly thirty years until my next visit to the United States.

As a postscript to the veterinary dream, sometime before my grandfather's ninetieth birthday, one of my cousins decided to inquire about that story and actually made contact with the Czech university that he studied in before the war. His records were found, and a few weeks later, the dean of the school of veterinary studies and the Czech ambassador to Israel came to Afikim and presented him with an honorary veterinary diploma. It got a headline in the major Israeli newspaper *Yediot Achronot*, and most of all, it made my grandfather a very happy old man.

CHAPTER 2

Innocence Interrupted

Surviving a Terrorist Attack

When I was eleven years old, I was nearly killed by Palestinian terrorists. I was out near the beach by myself, near the large agricultural fishponds where carp and tilapia (St. Peter's fish) were raised.

The heavy, swampy soil between the kibbutz and the sea was found to be unsuitable for farming. My grandparents and the other founding members of the kibbutz looked for a way to use this land, and someone came up with the idea of digging up the area and filling it, by running streams of water from a nearby brook, to form fishponds. This became a profitable industry for the kibbutz for decades. The operation is designed so that the fish reach marketable size around the Jewish holidays when the demand for fish is highest. Then the water is drained into the sea by specially designed pipes steering the flow through small canals. In those canals, we used to find and catch the smaller fish that had escaped the larger ponds.

I vividly remember the canal that widened into a small, round pond. The muddy sides of the pond were covered with reed and rush and other vegetation. The smell of mud and algae reeked of the swampy water. I loved playing in the ponds alone, daydreaming. I found an old fishing line with a hook and a wine bottle cork that served as a float; I tied it to a wooden stick, and it became my first fishing rod. Once in a while, I went fishing in the canals, usually catching small tilapia and then releasing them back into the water. The surrounding wildlife was captivating. There were storks and herons, gulls and other water birds; in the shallow water, there were various types of fish, tortoises, and water snakes. There was something mysterious and magical about this place, and yet it was also very familiar. It was around this time that I read Kenneth Grahame's *The Wind in the Willows* for the first time (I liked to read in English to keep up my language skills), and the wonderful riverside creatures described so artfully in the book sprang to life in front of me.

On a late Saturday afternoon in mid-March 1978, I went fishing, in one of those canals, near the beach. There was a strong, cool wind blowing in from the sea, and the high waves were crashing onto the beach. Clouds moved swiftly across the sky, and I began to feel chilly. I was sitting on the bank of one of the canals a couple of yards below the flat fishpond landscape, thus hidden from sight. I started fishing but after a while, I decided to go home and started to climb up the steep slope. As my head emerged slightly over the bush, I saw a group of men wearing camouflage uniforms, armed with AK-47 automatic rifles, moving toward me. I slowly retreated back down the bank of the canal. Instinctively I knew that something was not right here. Only many years later was I able to verbalize my understanding of what I had seen. I knew that Israeli soldiers do not engage in training exercises on Shabbat (Saturdays) and that most do not carry AK-47s. At the time I think it was just a gut feeling that made me hide. I moved slowly into the bush and held my breath. They passed a hair's breadth away from me. A few minutes later I heard the gunshots.

Later it was revealed that the terrorists had embarked on a large mother ship from the southern Lebanese Port of Tyre. They then transferred to rubber boats, intending to reach the beaches of Tel Aviv. After negotiating the rough sea, they lost their way and landed on the beach at my kibbutz – Maagan Michael, about thirty-five miles north of Tel Aviv. After passing by me in my hiding place, they encountered Gail Rubin, a young American woman. They interrogated her, and after she told them their location, they shot and killed her. Gail Rubin was a wildlife photographer. She worked with my grandmother at the Maagan Michael nature reserve and was out there not far from where I hid. She was known for her love of animals and human beings. Looking for an opportunity to capture the beauty of nature, she encountered the blind cruelty of terrorism.

The terrorists moved on, bypassed the kibbutz, and in an attempt to get to Tel Aviv, walked to the coastal road, where they stopped a bus, demanding that the driver head south toward their target, taking the driver and the passengers hostage. As they were driving, the terrorists shot at other cars on the road. By this time, an alert was out that a terrorist attack was in progress. Security forces near Herzliya, about five miles north of Tel Aviv, finally stopped the bus in a standoff that resulted in the deaths of many of the Israeli passengers who had been held hostage. This deadly attack, later dubbed the Coastal Road Massacre, was planned and launched by the Palestine Liberation Organization (PLO).

A large-scale Israeli military offensive against the PLO forces in Lebanon followed this horrific attack. Israeli ground forces stormed PLO bases in the south of Lebanon in retaliation and in order to deter future attacks. Little did I know at the time, but during this retaliatory raid, a young Israeli soldier, Reuven (Ruvik) Sarig, was killed. Ruvik was from Beit Haemek, a kibbutz located in the Western Galilee, not far from the Lebanese border. Ruvik, a communications trainee, volunteered to join the Golani infantry brigade that led the offensive into Lebanon. An improvised explosive device (IED) hit Ruvik's armored vehicle, killing him and three other soldiers. Years later I met Reuven's sister, Iris, who would later become my wife and the mother of our boys. On that fateful Saturday, our destinies collided. Ruvik's memory and the beautiful poetry and prose he left behind are ever present in our lives and in our hearts.

When I headed back to the kibbutz from the fishponds, I was surprised by all the activity and felt the tension around me. Men carrying guns were ordering the children to return to the children's houses and not to go outside. We were later moved to the second-floor apartments, which were easier to protect. It was not clear whether or not there were more terrorists in our area.

If You Want Peace, Prepare for War

Within hours, the tragic results of the attack became clear. Besides the terrible news about the bus attack on the outskirts of Tel Aviv, in which there were thirty-five dead and over seventy injured, Gail Rubin's body was found on the banks of one of the fishponds at the kibbutz. Three Zodiac rubber boats used by the attackers were found deserted on the beach along with two dead bodies, terrorists who had apparently drowned when one of their boats capsized.

The perception of our security changed dramatically: if it happened once, it could happen again. It was frightening, and we felt vulnerable.

For weeks after the attack, many items of military gear and ammunition continued to wash ashore. We children were drawn to the beach like magnets, hoping to find cool items such as commando knives. Every time a hand grenade or RPG anti-tank rocket washed ashore, we would report it to the grown-up kibbutz members, who would then call the police. We then waited to see the bomb squad in action. Controlled explosions were fun to watch. All of a sudden, I wasn't strolling on the beach looking for seashells. I was hoping to find different types of shells – ones that exploded and could kill.

It was a time of great uncertainty and angst. As I matured into my twelfth year, the notion and threat of another possible terrorist attack on our kibbutz became palpable in our community and in my own ruminations, especially at nights, trying to fall asleep in the children's house. It was scary and very real.

At that time, my father's infantry battalion, the military unit that he commanded in his reserve service, deployed along the northern Mediterranean coast and conducted patrols to prevent similar attacks. The same beach that I so loved, that was my childhood sanctuary, had turned into a frontier.

A few months later, Udi, my second brother, joined the family. Even then, years before I became a psychologist and became an expert at identifying grit, I saw his strong character and brilliant mind. Years later, he would excel in the Israeli Air Force and in business as well.

When I was fifteen, during the Jewish holidays, we set sail on a three-day excursion. Maritime navigation, sailing, and seamanship were an important part of our education. Every week, we had long afternoon sessions of seamanship training. During school vacations, longer cruises were the norm. In two small training sailboats, with a motorboat serving as chaperone, we left the kibbutz beach and headed north along the Mediterranean coast, toward Haifa. At the end of the long day, just before dusk, tired and wet after zigzagging against the wind, we finally entered the port of Haifa. Lowering the sails, we used our oars to maneuver the boats into a small and filthy industrial anchorage and tied the boats to one of the piers. As we were cooking dinner, a car from the kibbutz arrived. Our schoolteacher was in it. He called me over and congratulated me. He told me that I had a new baby sister.

Around that time, the kibbutz made the momentous decision to have babies and children move in with their parents. Growing up would be a very different experience for Tal, my sister. It is hard to imagine a more affectionate and emotionally connected person than my younger sister.

Around that time, at the age of fifteen, I joined the local special weapons and tactics (SWAT) team. The formation of SWAT teams in small, vulnerable communities was one of the measures taken following the Coastal Road Massacre. Many members on our kibbutz served in the special forces in the reserves; soon after the attack, a local SWAT fast-response team was formed. The idea was that in case of an attack, a fast and effective response team would be ready and only minutes – if not seconds – away. This preparedness could make the difference and thwart a massacre. The SWAT response team consisted of a sniper squad whose objective was to isolate the affected area; a tactical takeover team, assigned to storm the building where terrorists might be holding hostages and to engage them; and a small command headquarters, to manage the delicate situation. These local response SWAT teams were not, obviously, as professional and ready as the IDF's General Staff Reconnaissance Unit (Sayeret Matkal) or the YAMAM (the Israel Border Police SWAT unit). The idea was to act fast, try to avoid the attack, and isolate the area to prevent further casualties. The local SWAT team would deploy around the building where the hostages were held and would be ready to storm into it, if things deteriorated. Killing of hostages might necessitate a "go go go" response.

At that time, I had already started training at the shooting range with the dream of becoming an Olympic sharpshooter. I competed on the regional level. When I was competent enough, I was given an M-16 automatic rifle with a telescopic sight. I joined the snipers' squad. We felt we had to be prepared, so after completing my homework, every second week, I would join the SWAT team in counterterrorism training. A boy becomes a man early in Israel.

Holding a gun was an all-powerful feeling, and I experienced the urge to use it – to shoot. As an evolving humanist (or so I started to perceive myself back then), I found this urge troubling; it somehow didn't align with my moral values. Of course, the context was living at a time and in a place where one felt an existential threat and the need to protect and defend our home: *Si vis pacem, para bellum* (If you want peace, prepare for war). We had no choice but to be prepared in order to stop those whose goal it was to kill us.

In my case, at that time, holding a gun and feeling the excitement and the urge to use it was all the incentive I needed to lead me to seek action and combat. I was ready for the next chapter of my journey.

CHAPTER 3

A Boy Becomes a Man

The Recruitment Boot Camp

At eighteen, I joined the Shayetet – the Israeli Navy SEALs. In Israel, military service is mandatory, and having grown up in a military-oriented environment, I had the incentive to seek action, aim high, and serve in the elite special forces. The notion of stealth underwater attack and special operations resonated with my evolving manhood. In the summer of 1983, between the eleventh and twelfth grades, I took part in the Shayetet recruitment boot camp. Two hundred highly motivated young men, determined to succeed, reported to the Shayetet naval base. For a week, we were tested, pushed to our limits and beyond. In small teams, we were always wet, tired, running, or swimming and continuously scrutinized by trained SEAL veterans.

The water part was pretty easy for me. It was the natural habitat of my childhood. Diving into the water, holding my breath, I managed to successfully complete most of the tasks required of me. I collected objects from deep underwater, swam blindfolded and hit a target buoy a hundred yards away, and other tests. Late one night, we were given blindfolded diving masks and snorkels. We were instructed to stay in the water, face submerged, breathing through the snorkel while holding onto a rope, with a second rope below our feet. This exercise lasted for forty-five minutes in the pitch dark. All I could hear was the sound of my own breathing. Soon after the drill began, water started seeping into my mask. With my eyes tightly shut and salt water running into my nostrils, I sensed that I was not going to be able to stay underwater for much longer. Then I did what I was very good at – I detached myself. I had air to breathe through the snorkel, so I enjoyed the warm sea water and felt as if I had all the time in the world. When we were called to surface at the end of the drill, I heard that many of the other guys had found it very challenging. Some felt claustrophobic, panicked, and quit.

The running and other physical tasks were very challenging. At the kibbutz, summer meant walking barefoot most of the time. I didn't have real sneakers or hiking shoes, so I borrowed an old pair of army boots from a friend. I wasn't used to wearing them, let alone running in the deep sand, up and down dunes and in and out of the water, so blisters soon formed on my feet and toes. The pace was wicked, the summer heat and humidity unbearable. Not a natural athlete, I found it nearly impossible to keep on going.

This was the first time I had really challenged my own determination. It was about fighting that inner voice that was urging you to quit when the going became too hard and painful. It was about recruiting every ounce of motivation you never knew you had. I recall my back aching from carrying a backpack loaded with sand. My muscles ached and my spirit ached. Somehow I completed the long run on the last day of the camp. I was exhausted. We stopped for a rest, and our small group of boot camp "survivors" (eight or nine out of twenty-five who had started out on my team) was scattered in the shade, under an oak tree, somewhere on Mount Carmel.

Lying on my back, with an army hat covering my face, I was crying. I didn't know how much more we had to go through to complete this grueling boot camp. I was on the verge of giving up. The commander called us to stand up and get ready to go. I was hardly able to get up; my mind was foggy, and I felt confused and nearly hopeless. "I can't give up," I heard my inner voice say. "I can't go on," I retorted. "Guys, the screening is over," the commander said. "Good job! The bus will arrive shortly and take you all back to base."

It was such a great feeling and a huge relief. The next day, after a long psychological screening interview, I was accepted into the challenging SEAL training course.

That first psychological interview was, for me, a new and meaningful experience. Being able to reflect on what I had felt during the drills, answering questions on issues that I had never thought about, was intriguing. But mostly, I felt perplexed. It was unnerving and wonderful at the same time that someone could "look into my soul" and touch my inner sense of self.

Feeling a burst of self-esteem and anticipation about starting the long, difficult Shayetet training, I said my farewells to my new boot camp buddies and headed home. During the bus ride, I looked out the window and ruminated.

Dreams sometimes move people to action. For me, the participation and the success of passing the boot camp exercises created a new dream. I realized that I now wanted to become a Shayetet warrior more than anything else in the world.

Despite my sore, bloodied back from carrying a backpack full of sand and my blistered feet, I was elated. I got off the bus at the small junction about one mile from the kibbutz. It was early evening. Normally, I would walk this distance without thinking about it too much. With my army boots tied to my bag, I started walking barefoot toward home. The old asphalt road was boiling hot, so I stood there for a while in the shade of a tree, but no car came by. I started walking. One step at a time. I walked, almost meditating, smiling the pain away, accepting it, almost embracing the feeling of the moment. It was a long walk. Just before the kibbutz entrance, the road climbed toward a bridge that passed over the coastal road. I stopped for a moment, took a long look to my right, my eyes focusing on the exact place on the coastal road where, five years earlier, the terrorists had hijacked that bus. I remembered and thought about that day. It was an old habit. It was one of those external stimuli that ignite old memories and feelings. I continued walking over the bridge, already at the outskirts of the kibbutz, with only a few hundred yards left to go.

A car finally drove up beside me, driving into the kibbutz. I raised my hand, relieved that I would now enjoy riding the short (but painful) distance left. The car slowed down. The driver was Zaro.

General Meir Zorea, also known as Zaro, was a legendary figure. He was one of the founders of Maagan Michael. Zaro served in the Jewish Brigade of the British Army in World War II. He was part of a small group of Jewish officers who, like him, volunteered from Eretz Yisrael (the Land of Israel) to fight against the Nazis. After the war, when the terrible consequences of the Holocaust and the Nazi death machine were exposed, Zaro and a few other officers decided to take action. While the most senior Nazis were facing a military tribunal in Nuremberg, it became obvious that many former SS officers were out there and would escape justice. The SS was in charge of "the Final Solution to the Jewish problem." They were the group most responsible for executing six million Jews.

Many of these Jewish officers had lost their entire families in the Holocaust. This was their way to seek retribution. Using British Army trucks, guns, and supplies, Zaro and his men hunted Nazis who had gone underground. Under the radar, they captured former SS officers, death camp guards, and many others who were personally involved in the genocide conducted against the Jewish people. Some were shot or strangled on the spot. Others were interrogated for information about other Nazis who had taken part in the genocide effort and then executed.

I had only heard about "the Avengers" and about Zaro's leadership in these operations shortly before he pulled up next to me that evening. The story of the Avengers was not made public until the 1980s, decades after the war had ended. Zaro later became a high-ranking general in the IDF and a political leader. While he served as head of the IDF Northern Command, he would drive from his headquarters in northern Israel to meetings at the General Staff Headquarters in Tel Aviv. On the way, he would stop at the kibbutz, still dressed in military fatigues, board a tractor, and plow a field in order to regain his sense of connectedness to the land. His land.

Zaro and Naomi, his wife, had six sons. Two of them were killed in action while serving and defending Israel. Jonathan (Yoni) was a fighter pilot in the Israeli Air Force. On the first day of the 1967 Six-Day War, while attacking the Syrian airport in Damascus, his plane crashed into the Golan Heights. Yochanan (Yochik) served in the armored brigade. Six years after his brother, Yochik was killed during the 1973 Yom Kippur War, in an attempt to stop the Syrian tanks as they stormed the Golan Heights.

Zaro and Naomi's enormous sacrifice was palpable. As children, we heard stories about the wars and how Yoni and Yochik had been killed. Danny and Moshik, Zaro and Naomi's youngest twin boys, were my age and close friends of mine. Their loss was always present.

I was standing there with my sore feet, army boots hanging on my backpack, my hand extended seeking a ride. I smiled at Zaro, nodding my head in greeting. Zaro looked at me, his face displaying something like contempt. "Can't you walk such a short distance?" he said and drove away.

"Sure I can," I said to myself, puzzled. I walked the remaining distance to my room, having learned yet another lesson in coping.

End of School, Beginning of Love

Iris was born and raised on Kibbutz Beit Haemek, located in the Western Galilee, not far from the Lebanese border. We first met at her high school when she was a junior, just as she was going out for recess. Iris is eighteen months younger than I am. I was taking a gap year and did some educational work in her school and in some other schools in the area. The decision to take some time before enlisting in the military was not an easy one. I wanted to pursue my Shayetet dream but also to take some time, mature, and prepare myself for the line of duty. It was also the accepted norm on the kibbutz to volunteer in some capacity in the kibbutz movement or in underserved communities around the country. It turned out to be a life-changing year.

As a teenager, I was negotiating my way into adulthood. As a mostly detached young man, I was out there dating, exploring, and having fun. I most likely wasn't aware at the time, but what I really needed and was looking for was intimacy and love. I was looking for someone who could teach me what it means to care and feel. I needed a relationship. Iris turned out to be just that person.

She was standing there, outside the teachers' room, with a friend. She approached me and introduced herself. Years later, she told me that at that moment, she knew that I would be "her man." For my part, I did not have a clue. A few weeks later, we took off for a weekend trip to the desert. Against the picturesque scene of Wadi Qelt, a valley cutting through the Judean Mountains, near the stream that runs from Jerusalem to the Jordan Valley, our relationship became a reality. It took time, but she sensed that I could be reached and set free from those walls of detachment and emotional isolation. A new and exciting journey had begun. We started "going steady," and our relationship strengthened. We felt that we had to develop and stabilize the relationship before my enlistment. We knew it would be much harder when I was away.

I remember the first time I met her parents, in their small kibbutz apartment. They were ten or fifteen years older than my parents, a different generation. Pnina was a Sabra, a term used to describe those who were born in the Land of Israel. A *sabra* is the sweet but thorny fruit of a local cactus (prickly pear), which supposedly characterizes Israelis – prickly on the outside and sweet on the inside. She grew up on a moshav – a rural community of farmers. During the Second World War, Pnina's father had joined the Jewish Brigade in the British Army and went to fight the Nazis in North Africa and Europe. Pnina's mother could not manage the farm by herself, so as a young girl, Pnina took on many responsibilities in order to help provide for her family. It seems that this experience had been central in forming the hardworking and committed adult she became. She was rough at times, but caring and always engaged.

Max was born in Poland. As a child survivor of the Holocaust, he managed to flee with his mother from Nazi-held Poland into the area held by the Soviets. Max and his relatives were deported to Siberia, where they managed to stay together, enduring years of hardship, harsh winters, near starvation, and raging local anti-Semitism. His had been a family of means but was forced to leave everything behind, taking with them only some clothes and very few belongings. In an attempt to keep a family heirloom, Max hid an old, handmade gold watch that he had received from his grandmother in the heel of his shoe. For years, the watch remained hidden. When the war was over, and the heel of his worn-out shoe was opened, he found that the watch was completely crushed. Max kept the ruined watch, and many years later, that same gold was melted down by a goldsmith and was used by Iris and myself to make our wedding rings.

After a long journey by train and by foot, Max returned to his Polish hometown only to discover that most of his family members had perished. As soon as it became possible, he emigrated to the young State of Israel and enlisted in the IDF. He had to learn Hebrew, the new Sabra culture, try to blend in and become a soldier. He met Pnina after he had completed his military service.

Caring and accepting, they opened their arms and hearts to me. I was puzzled when I realized how different Iris's home was from my own. Max and Pnina were central figures in their community. They were old school and not very verbal. But in their presence, I experienced something new. There was a sense of sadness and loss, their longing for Ruvik – their fallen son – evident. There was also a strong, almost ideological sense that life must go on. Iris's home became the context in which we developed as individuals and as a couple.

With our relationship newly forming, I completed my gap year. In the summer of 1985, I was ready to put on a uniform and start the long journey of serving my country.

PART TWO
SHAYETET 13 – THE ISRAELI NAVY SEALs

Like the AK-47, I did not stop, nor did I miss my target. I became a fighting machine. The strength of steel, however, comes at the expense of flexibility. I lost the remains of my inner tenderness.

CHAPTER 4

Cultivating the Warrior Mentality

Becoming a Soldier

I served in the Shayetet for more than twenty years. I began as a warrior, then was an operational commander, and later I became the unit's psychologist. Over the years, the areas of my responsibility evolved from leading men in combat to building their psychological resilience and fighting capacity to caring for their well-being. Connecting these domains of expertise – of military special operations, counterterrorism, combat diving, and the ability to lead men into battle with the realms of the human mind and spirit, understanding stress, behavior, and leadership – these uncommon connections became the foundation on which I have built my career.

The first years of my operational tenure could be defined as a long swim, an ongoing dive with countless physical exercises, extensive operational training, and many combat missions.

Being amphibian has a price. The first part of the program was the standard IDF infantry basic training. The hard part of becoming a soldier is not necessarily the physical component of running and carrying heavy combat gear; it is not learning to shoot, navigate, or win battles; it is the process itself in which you are transformed from a happy, carefree teenager into a mature soldier who must risk his or her life in the course of duty.

In the southern Negev Desert, far from the sea, our small group of Shayetet trainees was stationed with a Paratroopers battalion. The Israeli Paratroopers Brigade has a long tradition of professionalism and an ethos of courage and determination. This was the place in which we would set out on the painful journey to becoming soldiers.

Our base had about twenty large tents, loads of dust, and a boiling hot August sun, a few sergeants who challenged us, and pretty much nothing else. That was to be our home for the coming six months.

Our daily routine was as follows: wake-up call at five a.m., training and drilling late into the night. You come to learn a new language, a new way of thinking, and a very different way of being. Standing in formation, wearing a uniform, and obeying orders, constantly being harassed by our sergeant, getting used to the new army boots, blisters forming on every toe, one quickly loses one's sense of self.

Social psychology describes this process as deindividuation, necessary in the preparedness to military fighting capacity. You must give up some of your autonomy and identity in order to be able to fight, in order to be able to kill and to face the possibility of getting killed.

I remember feeling peculiar in my new surroundings and life. At first it felt like a game. Then it became something much more intense. Immersed in this process, without any privacy or time to reflect, I started losing the inner sense of who I was. I knew I wanted to be a Navy SEAL, and I knew I was Yotam, an eighteen-year-old who had recently enlisted, who had friends and family and an inner world. But now it all felt vague and distant. I was gasping for air and for a meaning to fuel my inner struggle to survive. The feeling was threatening and pushed me to experience parts of my inner self that were new to me.

I remember writing a letter home in which I described my situation using an analogy of me as a tiny microorganism that was being swallowed up by an enormous amoeba. That was how it felt. My father wrote back, trying to put my situation into context with a rather moral, ethical, and value-driven talk: Zionism, nation building, defense. He was an experienced fighter, a reserve battalion commander, holding the rank of lieutenant colonel. I was a newly enlisted private in basic training. He was my father. I was his son. It was as if we were speaking two different languages. We understood each other perfectly but had no idea what the other was talking about.

A few weeks later, I felt something new starting to take shape inside me. I was emerging from this transformative cocoon with a new sense of my own identity, with layers of toughness and maturity. When I arrived home for a Shabbat leave, Iris had hitchhiked the long way from her kibbutz and was waiting for me to arrive. We had been serious for over a year by then, so being separated was hard on both of us. We hugged and kissed in the doorway. She then looked at me with her clever, penetrating, and loving eyes and said I looked different. She was aware that I had undergone a change and that I seemed older and more mature. Something had changed in my eyes, and she saw it.

The Founding Fathers

Sea, air, and land. This is the meaning of the acronym SEAL. The US Navy SEALs are probably the best and most capable military special forces unit in the world. In Israel, we call our equivalent naval special warfare unit Shayetet 13 and view ourselves as second to none. The Hebrew word *shayetet* can be translated as "flotilla," a group of ships or boats. In the Israeli Navy, the various flotillas comprise Shayetet 3 (the Missile Boats Flotilla), Shayetet 7 (the Submarine Flotilla), and Shayetet 13 (Naval Special Operations). Sharing similar evolutionary paths, the US Navy SEALs and Shayetet 13 have, over the years, moved away from mainly underwater demolition, stealth combat dives, and sea-based ground raids on enemy targets to performing tactically complicated and dangerous land operations, some with the highest strategic importance.

In the mid-1940s, after the end of World War II, thousands of Jewish Holocaust survivors attempted to reach the safe haven of British-occupied Palestine – Eretz Yisrael. Many were intercepted by the British Royal Navy and sent back to Europe or were held in detention camps either on the island of Cyprus or near the coastal Israeli town of Atlit, close to where the Shayetet's base is today. The Holy Land (Eretz Yisrael) was at that time under British Mandate, granted by the League of Nations after the First World War. The British did not allow Jews to emigrate freely to their ancient homeland, and an underground struggle unfolded during the 1940s in which the local Jewish population was determined to rescue Holocaust survivors. They smuggled these refugees onto Eretz Yisrael's shores while preparing for Israel's declaration of independence and for the war that would surely follow.

The struggle was not only underground but also on and under the water. Years before Israel's independence, a few brave men swam and dove in the dangerous waters of British naval bases in several Mediterranean ports and sabotaged Royal Navy destroyers and ships with improvised limpet mines. Spearheading the "illegal" immigration as part of the establishment of the

State of Israel and taking responsibility for rescuing survivors were the founding fathers of Shayetet 13. Two of them, Yohai Ben-Nun and Yosef (Yossele) Dror were the leaders of the evolving unit.

Yohai was awarded the highest medal of honor for bravery for his part in the operation of sinking the Egyptian Navy's flagship, the *Emir Farouk*. During Israel's War of Independence, rigging small boats with explosives, the team closed in on the heavily armed destroyer. After the destroyer was hit, Yohai made a final assault on a smaller Egyptian warship that had detected the team and was bearing down on it. Risking his own life to ensure the success of the mission while under heavy enemy fire, Yohai attacked the larger vessel and managed to jump off his boat at the last second before it hit its target and exploded. He saved the lives of his fellow teammates and set high standards for us all as a leader. He later became an admiral and head of the Israeli Navy.

Yossele Dror created and commanded the underwater demolition team which, many years later, I was privileged to command. Yossele foresaw that the young Israeli state required strategic assets to defend itself, including long-range underwater naval capabilities. He envisioned and later established the Israeli Submarine Flotilla and became its first commander.

These two exceptional, innovative, and brave men were members of Kibbutz Maagan Michael, where I was born and raised, and, needless to say, were role models and an inspiration to me. Yohai shared his stories and advice with me when I was training with the Shayetet. When I became an officer and team leader, he always showed an interest and offered priceless advice on leadership issues.

Yossele died tragically in the mid-1970s when I was a young boy. After retiring from active duty, he joined the Israeli merchant fleet and "sailed the seven seas." He was a gifted storyteller; his stories and letters were published posthumously. When I was a teenager, I read his books and imagined an inner dialogue that I shared with this exceptional man. The combination of courage, bravery, and soulfulness, along with his ability to write and create, really touched me. Yossele was in his fifties when he fell to his death during a tour on the volcanic island of Stromboli, Sicily. Fifteen years later, doing security work on an Italian pleasure liner, I sailed past Stromboli. I stood on the command bridge with a sense of emotional anticipation as I followed the ship's route on the nautical maps and viewed with my own eyes the place where he died. I stood on the ship's starboard watch in the cool breeze as I glimpsed the dark volcanic rock. It was a moment of closure, another circle of shared history charged with personal meaning.

In the shadow of these giants, I felt great responsibility but also pride in our shared raison d'être: to be entrusted with this position and to take part in this important chapter in the history of our nation. Little by little, my mission began to unfold.

Amphibians, Lean and Mean

There was still so much work to do. The Shayetet training course was long, tough, and challenging. After completing basic training, we reported to the Atlit Naval Base, just a few miles south of the city of Haifa, Israel's northern metropolis. A few miles west of the Carmel Mountain on the Mediterranean coastal plain and a few miles north of Maagan Michael, the base is situated near a picturesque natural bay. Atlit Bay became my second home for the next twenty years. Its sandy beaches stretch from the base and its facilities to the ruins of a Crusader castle, standing as a silent witness to the medieval presence of the Knights Templar, who took part in the European quest to conquer the Holy Land.

The Crusaders were strong, heavily armed, and known for their fortifications. Their Muslim enemies were lean and fast. In an iconic battle that took place in 1187 CE at Hattin, a volcanic high ground just west of the Sea of Galilee, Saladin, the Muslim warlord, took advantage of the Crusaders' weakness. The heavily armored Crusader knights were lured into battle in the July sun and quickly became dehydrated and exhausted as they roasted inside their armor; they were easily defeated by the Arab warriors.

The modern-day global Jihad ideologists Osama bin Laden and Ayman al-Zawahiri (founders of Al Qaeda), as well as Abu Bakr al-Baghdadi (founder of ISIS) have exploited this story as an analogy of their struggle against what they refer to as Western colonialism. In the asymmetrical power struggle between radical Islam and the West, they saw themselves as today's version of Saladin facing the Western Crusaders. It is symbolic that both bin Laden and al-Baghdadi were killed by US special forces – the lean and mean operational arm of the modern-day superpower.

I believe that the lesson history teaches Israelis is that we must not only be lean and fast, but agile and always proactively adjusting to change. As human beings, we long for the elusive vision of peace and stability. The truth we often deny is that in today's world, change is constant and indeed against our nature, and it is a challenge to reinvent ourselves over and over. Adapting to change improves the chances of surviving and thriving. Proactively initiating change and forming a new reality allows you to excel and flourish and take control of your destiny.

During that cold winter and early spring of 1986, in the challenging Shayetet training course, in the shadow of the ancient Crusader castle, these ideas about modern warfare were perhaps only scattered thoughts in my tortured being.

CHAPTER 5

Getting through BUD/S Training

The Only Easy Day Was Yesterday

Long weeks, longer days and nights, never-ending hours of hard, cold, painful, and challenging drills were all taken a minute at a time. We started each day with a swim in the Mediterranean water, followed by intense physical training, long runs, longer swims, and operational amphibious warfare exercises: seaborne raids, counterterror and reconnaissance training, learning to operate Zodiac rubber boats, weapons training, and much, much more.

Schedules were designed in such a way that from the second you were awoken in the morning until you fell exhausted into a deep sleep late at night, you had entered the fast lane of drills and exercises. There was no downtime. Not a minute wasted.

Assembling the Zodiac Mark V rubber boats, we would work very fast while one of us – the trainee in charge – would shout every now and then: "Two minutes to go!" And then, "Stand in formation!" If the boat was not ready on time, if a motor or gasoline tank was not properly tied, or if one of many small details was not perfectly executed, we would get a seven-minute run to submerge ourselves in the sea water. Seven minutes is just about the time it takes to undress, run into the water, get completely wet, run back to find your clothes, and get dressed. Those who didn't make it on time would get a second call. Then a third. After that, the time was decreased to four minutes, which meant that you had to get into the water fully dressed in fatigues and boots. When our SEAL trainers became especially creative, they would command us to roll in the sand and turn into "schnitzels" or "sugar cookies."

Once the boats were ready, it was time to carry them from the boathouse to the water. A Zodiac Mark V with two outboard engines, floorboards, four tanks of gas, oars, an anchor, a watertight wireless radio, and basic navigation equipment weighed around two thousand pounds. For a small group of Shayetet trainees, this is a heavy payload to lift and carry. The thing is, it is not sufficient to be strong enough to lift the boat. You have to believe that you can do it, and your teammates have to believe it too. Then a shout is given: "Eh op!" and the boat is hoisted up and carried away toward the water.

In the deep sand, the soles of the military boots sink, making the journey even more arduous. Backs ache as the dark, inflated rubber boat weighs down on our shoulders. The dark rubber, resting on my shoulder, also presses against my ear. Heated in the winter sun, I feel the comforting warmth of the rubber boat. In a few minutes, it will be very cold. My boots are sinking into the deep sand. I can hear my team members, encouraging one another. As we make progress toward the water, the sand becomes wet, hard, compressed. It's easier to walk, and we start running with the Zodiac as if it's taking flight. Finally, the boat reaches the water and is lowered slowly, with the bow floating on the water.

When the command is given, the boat is lifted to waist level and hoisted into the sea. While the team jumps onto the boat and gets the engines started, I would usually remain standing in the deep water, holding the bow until the boat was ready to go. This means that even before the training session began, I was already totally wet. In a few minutes, so was everybody else. Learning the basics of handling a boat, navigating it, and conducting maneuvers, one of us manned the steering wheel. The rest of the team would sit on the inflated sides of the boat and do their best not to fall asleep. That was an almost impossible task. Sleep deprivation is a biological state that overcomes you and gets you against your will. One after the other, our heads would nod down, eyes rolling and closing. Then the inevitable shout from the sergeant would shake you: "Yotam, are you sleeping?" After this, the sergeant would signal by a nod of his head, pointing overboard, a gesture meaning, "Off you go." Falling back into the cool water was an unpleasant but invigorating experience. It would normally keep me awake for a few minutes, until the next time.

In this constant state of activity, training and struggling, most of us were clearly detached, focusing on the task at hand. At times, I would force myself to lift my eyes, to look at the Mediterranean horizon, the setting sun, or the lights of Haifa, Atlit, and sometimes, when visibility allowed, the lights of Maagan Michael – my home kibbutz, not so far off.

One by one, many of my teammates gave up and left the unit. Others were found to be incompetent by our staff and were ordered to leave. One day they were with us, laughing and joking, biting their lips in training, and the next day they were gone. I had my own moments of nearly giving up. I had to somehow dig deep and keep on going, pushing hard. At times it seemed nearly impossible. Of the sixty-eight who started basic training, only sixteen made it to the end of this training phase.

Many years later, when I visited the Naval Special Warfare Center in Coronado, California, I was struck by the similarities between the two units – the US Navy SEALs and the Israeli Shayetet. Both evolved along the same path. The US Navy Basic Underwater Demolition/SEALs (BUD/S) basic training is probably the hardest and most notorious of all special operations units. The Israeli Shayetet *mechin* (Hebrew for prep stage) basic training is just as challenging.

As the weeks passed, we carried more weight, walked, ran, and swam longer distances. We challenged our willpower to endure in ways we thought were impossible. Always wet with either sweat or saltwater (sometimes both), with blisters on every toe, we endured what was at times unbearable pain. My muscles ached, my bones ached, but more than anything, my core being hurt like hell. Pain and fatigue challenge your stamina, screaming at you that you can't go on.

When inner voices are trying to rationalize that what you're doing is too hard to bear, that is the point when you persuade yourself that you don't really want this. This is what happens to many in the face of these ultra-demanding training drills, leading them to declare that they "don't really want this anymore." Only after leaving do some regain their will, but it is too late. Often a young Shayetet training candidate, about to participate in the recruitment boot camp, would ask for my advice, for tips on how to succeed. The only words of wisdom I can offer are to never listen to those inner voices at the peak of an unbearable situation. Endure until you can reach a break and catch your breath. Hold on until the end of the hour, the day, the week. Think again and reconnect to your internal determination.

Care for Your Combat Gear and It Will Serve You

During the first week of the Shayetet *mechin* BUD/S training, the notorious land-to-sea basic training, I became acquainted with my new companion, my extra limb – I could almost say my significant other: my AK-47.

The AK-47, also known as the Kalashnikov, is a Soviet assault rifle, initially developed in the 1940s. It has become one of the most widely used weapons in the world. It is massive and heavy, but its simple mechanism enables firing, without jamming, under almost any condition. Its ammunition is waterproof, so it is the perfect sea-to-land rifle. It isn't a very accurate shot, but I became so attached to this piece of Russian steel that I knew I could count on it to serve me well and perhaps save my life if the occasion arose.

Our daily routine included cleaning our living quarters, shaving, polishing our boots, and cleaning our rifles. That same Russian steel that performed so well also had a disturbing quality: when immersed in seawater, it would oxidize and rust in a matter of minutes, faster than other similar weapons. Most military weapons are treated by a process of browning, which helps prevent corrosion. These AK-47s were immersed in the sea so frequently that the dark surface eroded and appeared white and shiny, rusting quickly. During operations, dark spray paint was used to camouflage these rifles.

Every morning, using kerosene and gun oil, I would scrub and fight the rust, knowing that any red spot – or freckles, as we called them – left untreated might cost me another mile of running. This punishment was meant to remind us "through the legs" what it takes to be a fighter in the Shayetet, to become a Navy SEAL. It was the old-school way to teach us the importance of taking good care of our combat gear. Care for your combat gear, and it will serve you.

Each one of us had a large, personal storage locker near the barracks where all our combat gear was kept – wet suits, fins, special raiding boots, a fully equipped raiding vest, and a buoyancy belt to keep you floating with all of this heavy gear in tow.

Training schedules were never provided in advance. Each day, each hour, sometimes minute by minute, an order would be given to be ready for the next training session. Usually within minutes, you had to run and get your raiding gear ready. The challenge was to put everything together and make sure nothing was missing, to double-check that all the pieces of equipment – from the commando knife to the flare gun and AK-47 – were neatly secured to the vest, so that once in the water or on land, nothing would be lost. In training, it was not an issue. In future operational work, leaving suspicious traces in enemy territory might expose our presence there. We did not want this to happen.

After running around during the intensive preparation to get the combat gear ready, we would stand in formation, dressed in wetsuits under our uniforms, vests holding magazines full of rounds, AK-47s hanging, strapped on shoulders. Sweat would mix with the salty sea water, dripping from the gear, still wet from a previous exercise. An instructor would then check each soldier, making sure all was in place. In this final check, any minor breach – an untied string, a loose end in the raiding gear – would be noted, to be paid for later.

When the order was given, the team would walk into the water, fins in hand. Inflating the buoyancy belt, we would then lean back into the water and mount the fins on our boots, strapping them behind the heels. Swimming in full raiding gear is a hard task. We would stay in formation, stealthily approaching the dark predetermined landing beach. Swimming was laborious, and we had to ensure that the fins didn't break the surface of the water, because stealth requires that no white foam or unnecessary water turbulence be visible. Hitting the ground as the water became shallow, we had to learn the necessary drills of transforming from swimming mode, totally submerged, heads just above water, to an effective strike force once on land. Removing the fins from our boots, we'd tie them to the vest and move silently inland.

As the weeks passed, we were given additional weapons and combat gear. Pretty soon I was swimming with an even heavier and bigger companion: an FN MAG 58 machine gun, carrying chains of hundreds of rounds in a special watertight backpack. This additional firepower, along with the rocket-propelled grenades (RPGs) and light anti-tank weapons (LAW missiles) that my team members carried, was essential in some operational scenarios. Each one of us had his own team weapon to carry. And to clean, oil, and care for, once training was over, usually late at night.

As training progressed, I substituted the Belgian MAG for a Russian PK light machine gun. This was a powerful, accurate, and mean piece of hardware. In order to operate it, strong arms and shoulders were required, as well as kick-ass determination.

Before each meal, outside the unit's pantry and dining hall, we would gather and stand in formation, running to be there on time. Each soldier would then have to climb a twenty-foot rope and place all five fingers on the branch of a Eucalyptus tree it was tied to. For the machine gun operators, rope climbing was not enough. We needed to develop and strengthen the muscles of our shoulders and arms. Therefore, a handful of us who had the privilege of being machine gunners also had to exercise cocking the MAG and PK dozens of times before each meal.

Full Combat Gear March – The *Masa'ot*

Physical training is a central part of Navy SEAL training. Beyond the long runs and swims, with or without fins, and the heavy boats that we carried, there was a special, almost mythological relevance to the *masa'ot*. *Masa* (plural *masa'ot*) means march but carries the connotation of a journey. This was the term commonly used in the military for long runs in full combat gear, carrying a heavy backpack full of sand and, at times, hoisting an open stretcher with one of our comrades aboard. During these *masa'ot*, the iron warriors are forged into steel. The pace was always fast, wicked. Every week the *masa'ot* became longer, running in deep sand, the weight carried becoming progressively heavier. At the end of BUD/S, we had to run a fifty-five-mile *masa*, from Tel Aviv to the Atlit Naval Base. It was a grueling test.

About a year after my enlistment and nearly halfway through the Shayetet training course, this fifty-five-mile *masa* represented an important (and dreaded) milestone. Historically, there were always guys who did not manage to complete it. Some fainted during the last few miles, their psyches giving in to the limits of their physical bodies. Others gave up, saying they just couldn't go on. A few were taken to the hospital's emergency room and returned with casts on their broken legs.

In a carefully designed preparation process, the distance run and weight carried were gradually raised with each *masa*. Back in the 1980s, there was a lack of awareness regarding the importance of proper nutrition and getting enough sleep. Even the strongest motivation and stamina cannot bend the rules of physics and biology. The body needs all of its available energy to keep on going. The bones need rest and healing time, which is attained during sleep. At that time, we were getting only three or four hours of sleep each night, and that was not enough.

As the *masa'ot* grew longer, I also started to worry about my army boots. The same boots that cut through my feet in basic training became soft and accommodated the shape of my feet. With the now substantial mileage traveled, they started to disintegrate, and it looked like I would have to switch to new ones just before the final *masa*. I was terrified every day to see new holes appear, the leather stretching and cracks beginning to appear in the rubber soles of the boots. About two weeks before showtime, I had to make a tough decision. At home, on my Shabbat leave, I took the new pair of boots I had and gave them a persuasive session. With a heavy hammer, I systematically beat the new leather in order to soften them. I tried every trick in the book; I had to.

After an atypical long night's sleep, we had our gear ready: AK-47s, personal vests with ammo, a flare gun, two canteens of water, a commando knife, a diving flashlight, and a medical first-aid kit. Oh, yes, and a backpack full of a heavy payload of sand. We also had the team gear to carry: two stretchers, additional water, and a radio. We boarded an old truck and started the drive to Tel Aviv.

It was August, and the Israeli summer weather was hot and humid. The beach was packed with regular people, enjoying an afternoon at the beach. We got off the truck and stood in formation, ready to go. Looking down at my shiny new boots, I wiggled my toes and noted that the leather felt hard and unforgiving. "This is going to be hard," I said to myself, and to Gidi, a teammate who by then had become a close friend. We had been together since basic training. He put his hand on my shoulder and said, "You can do it." I just had to believe him. I had to believe in myself.

The first few hours were tough but tolerable. I detached myself, concentrating on the heels of those running in front of me. As it became dark and the miles started to accumulate, I started to grasp just how dire my situation was becoming. The leather was eating its way into my flesh. Pain was building up, and both feet hurt terribly. At one of the stops, during a ten-minute break for water, I made the mistake of taking my boots off. I saw huge blisters, open and bleeding, burning and painful. At this stage, it became hard for me to keep up the pace. My buddies had to help me, and a "tow kit" – namely, a short rope – was used to tie me to two of the stronger guys. I held onto the rope, doing my best. By midnight, we passed Maagan Michael. The dark beach looked so familiar but also different. I was in such pain, I was crying silently. The lights of my kibbutz, my room were so close by, and yet so far away.

We kept on running in silence. Every now and then some shouts of encouragement could be heard. At first light, we could see the Shayetet base. It gave me a new burst of energy, and even though the pain was at its peak,

I felt that I was almost flying, probably on the remnants of my physical and mental energy.

By this time, three guys had quit the *masa*. During the breaks, we saw them sitting in the accompanying command car looking sad and defeated. They knew they would have to repeat and complete the *masa* from the beginning.

We entered the base and ran to the barracks. Just near our rooms stood an old water tower, formerly used for diving training. We ran up the stairs leading all the way up and congregated on the roof of the tower. The view of the Bay of Atlit was breathtaking. The sense of accomplishment was huge. Upon command, we all took out our flare guns, loaded flares, and shot them into the sky. The *mechin* – the first, notorious phase of BUD/S – was over.

CHAPTER 6

Relationships

The Art of Detachment

Throughout those long night runs, swims, and operational exercises, I could feel my stamina and determination building and felt encouraged. It was proof of my growing physical fitness and newly acquired fighting skills together that boosted my sense of self-worth and capability. But that was not the whole story: the mental component of this toughening-up experience required an inner psyche change. Based on my early childhood on the kibbutz and the defense mechanisms I had developed, I quickly relearned the art of detachment, entering a state of being that had little room for feelings or emotions. This ability helped me cope with the reality of my shrinking team: my newly acquired buddies, to whom I had become attached, trickled out of the unit. But my fortitude came at a price. Like forged Russian steel, I became stronger, tougher, and functioned better. Like the AK-47, I did not stop, nor did I miss my target. I became a fighting machine. The strength of steel, however, comes at the expense of flexibility. I lost the remains of my inner tenderness.

It became harder and harder to feel, to love, to be emotionally present in my intimate relationship with Iris. Looking back on those intense times, I can only admire how patient and accepting she was toward this detached stallion that I had become, hoping, perhaps knowing that I would someday become emotionally reborn. It took years, but she was willing to wait. Along the way, I questioned the whole relationship. Looking back, I now know that I was scared of opening up, of enabling my emotions to surface. I was starting to feel a new, perhaps threatening emotion. For the first time in my life, I was in love. To this day, I carry with me the sorrow and regret that in the spring of 1987, a few months after graduating the grueling Shayetet course, about three years into our relationship, I broke up with her.

It was after I had told her, for the first time, that I loved her. I remember how I had nearly panicked. I was not able to verbalize it at the time, but lowering my defenses, letting go of my emotional detachment, was probably something that I just could not afford to do at this point of my life.

It was a miserable time for both of us. We licked our wounds, dated others, and desperately tried to understand why this had happened to us. To make matters worse, I was on a complete ego trip, feeling as if I had conquered the world upon achieving my Shayetet dream. The realization that I had been off course came pretty quickly, and I gently asked Iris to forgive my stupidity and take me back. Luckily, she said yes. We were together again, both of us feeling that this was it.

Mentors

Given my Spartan upbringing on the kibbutz, with so little interaction with my parents and siblings, I have often wondered, especially after becoming a parent myself, how I survived communal living emotionally. My parents were the first generation to be raised on a kibbutz. They lacked much of the primary experience that we today consider the basics of "good-enough" parenting to enable emotional stability in their children. They were doing what they understood was right, but were mostly busy with kibbutz matters and with themselves. I was out there, strolling around with my peers, taking long walks around the fishponds near the kibbutz. I was a curious and polite child and was referred to as the "responsible adult," always accountable. At the age of five, I was nicknamed the *mem peh*, the Hebrew abbreviation for *mefaked plugah* (company commander). I was happy and self-confident, albeit somewhat emotionally detached, even back then.

Many years later, I acknowledged two figures who were significant to me in my early childhood. They were very different, and each compensated for a place that I didn't even know was missing – a sense of familial closeness.

Judith Kramer Ayalon, my grandmother, was born in Riga, Latvia, two decades after the turn of the twentieth century. She emigrated to British Mandate Palestine (Eretz Yisrael) as a young girl and settled in the northern city of Haifa with her parents. In 1936, there were many armed assaults against the Jewish population, during a period of unrest that became known as the Arab rebellion. Palestinians began their uprising against British troops and the Jewish population. In one of those attacks, Judith's father, my great-grandfather, was killed by a bomb that exploded on a bus. Her mother, Gita, was heartbroken and in dire straits and could not provide for her only daughter. So Judith went to live with her cousin. She had to grow up fast and take control of her life.

In her late teens, a group of young adults in her youth movement (Hatzofim, the Hebrew Scouts) sought to establish a new kibbutz. Prior to settling near the Mediterranean beach, they trained, studied, and practiced communal life on a small hillside near the city of Rehovot, adjacent to the Weizmann Institute of Science. In Rehovot, Judith and her comrades engaged in a secret and dangerous mission, manufacturing 9mm rounds for submachine guns, in anticipation of the coming invasion that was bound to follow Israel's declaration of independence. The neighboring Arab countries repeatedly threatened to annihilate the new state.

This secret factory, the Ayalon Institute, was named after the biblical Valley of Ayalon. According to the story in the Bible, the Israelites fought the Amorites and in order to win, they needed to prolong the daylight hours. "Then Joshua spoke to the Lord in the day when the Lord delivered up the Amorites before the children of Israel, and he said in the sight of Israel, 'Sun, stand still at Givon, and you moon in the Valley of Ayalon'" (Joshua 10:12). This tactical advantage enabled the Israelites to maximize their victory.

At the Ayalon Institute, over four million 9mm rounds were manufactured during the first months of Israel's War of Independence. This ammunition proved to be critical to the survival of the newborn state.

A small group of members who shared the secret worked around the clock. They would sneak into the kibbutz laundry room and move an industrial-sized washing machine that covered the entrance to a tunnel leading to their makeshift factory, eight yards below ground. Risking their lives and freedom, they worked in total secrecy for close to three years. Any breach of secrecy could have led to their arrest by the British. Any minor mistake or technical fault could have easily caused an explosion and their death. This is another story of the unsung heroes of Israel's fight for independence.

After the State of Israel was founded, the group settled on the hillside near the Mediterranean, where Maagan Michael remains today. Judith became a biology teacher, an expert in the wildlife surrounding the kibbutz, and a beloved figure to her students and colleagues. In her late eighties, her mind was still crystal clear, she was healthy and still working, lecturing, and holding on to firm opinions on current issues. For me, she was Grandmother. She played a special role in my life and always seemed to be present and available for me, both intellectually (teaching me about the local flora and fauna) and emotionally, even though she was not considered an expressive person. She gave me the attention I needed.

I would stroll around as a young boy, and my path would lead to the old lab where she worked. She gave me small containers to collect my findings: small fish or algae, insects, or plants. She was not excessively warm, but she was very accepting. She was present and connected without being gushy. She passed away at ninety, peacefully migrating to other worlds, a little like the birds that passed over our region in the autumn and again in the spring. They would pause near the kibbutz, giving her the chance to see this marvel of nature up close.

In retrospect, I identified another figure from my past who, I believe, had a major role in who I was to become. She was warm, loving, and tender. Early childhood memories, recalled in black and white photographs, appeared before me. I can remember her deep eyes and her unconditional acceptance. I would crawl up to her before I learned to walk. I demanded her attention and got it, even when she had crawling offspring of her own. Riah was our German shepherd. She was in tune with me and cared for me as if I were her puppy. I have always had a natural ease with dogs. To this day, I never fear them, easily find channels of communication with them, and enjoy their closeness, petting and stroking their fur.

When I think about the figures who influenced my childhood and with whom I felt a close connection, I naturally think of Savta Judith's special presence and guidance as well as a deep sense of connection with Riah. All of the other relationships from my childhood compelled me into survival mode. Within the pack at the children's house, my classmates or alternative siblings and I somehow managed our lives in a relatively autonomous society. Some were strong, some weak. Some were competitive in life and in play, taking advantage of others. Even children in this supposedly idyllic setting could sometimes be cruel.

I cannot say that I had a bad childhood. I was not beaten or abused, nor was I deprived intentionally of any material or spiritual need. The kibbutz, an experimental and ideological society, believed that it was doing its best when it came to nurturing its offspring. The idea behind communal living as opposed to being raised in a family was that raising children in a non-parental environment by trained caregivers would produce a different and perhaps better outcome. In a sense, they were right. This modern-day Sparta produced an amazingly disproportionate percentage of "New Israelis," serving as fighter pilots, armored brigade commanders, and infantry officers as well as in other elite units. It was a pipeline for the *right stuff*, so essential to the young nation living constantly under threat. It was us, the children of the big communal experiment, who were ready and eager to go and do our part. In retrospect, I paid a price: an emotional numbness, a crippling and distorted interpersonal ability, being out of reach and out of touch.

The Operational Team

Operations are usually conducted on dark, moonless nights. The Shayetet's battle procedure includes a careful analysis of the landing beach, monitoring of enemy activity in the area, and operational planning. The team chosen to execute the mission prepares the combat gear, is briefed extensively, and conducts training. We aim to reach peak performance on the day of the operation.

The gear is checked and rechecked, and final details and changes in the operational plan are briefed. The warriors, in the SEAL delivery boats, move swiftly across the water, far from the enemy shore. As the sun sets, the boats penetrate into well-guarded enemy waters. When the shore becomes visible, the boats slow down, in tight formation. With the use of night-vision gear, the beach is screened for unwanted presence – an enemy patrol, a pickup truck carrying a heavy machine gun – anything that might challenge the silent attackers. A hand signal is given, and the men put on their fins and silently get off the boats, slipping into the water. In seconds, the team converges and swims in formation, the team leader in the center of the line of warriors.

The soldiers are in full combat gear, uniform worn over wetsuit, a vest with thirty-round AK-47 magazines, hand grenades, and communication gear. The warriors swim on their backs, heading toward the dark beach. Swimming becomes laborious with fins on your boots while holding an AK-47. Breathing is difficult, since nearly the entire body is submerged. The lungs are below the surface, water pressure building around them. Leg muscles ache as the team approaches the shore. After pausing to observe the surroundings, making sure that there is no one else around, the warriors hit the ground in shallow water and slowly advance toward the beach. Fins are removed and fastened by their back straps onto the wrist of the dominant hand, which is also clutching the Kalashnikov, forefinger on the trigger, in readiness. Dark, camouflaged faces are barely visible, tired eyes staring into the dark. The team emerges from the sea onto enemy shore.

After stealthily walking the short distance from the waves washing ashore toward the low brush, indicating dry land, the team stops. Each soldier finds a dark spot, kneels down, and quickly attaches the fins to special straps on the side of his vest as he gets ready for the next phase, whether it be a stealth reconnaissance mission, an assault on a terrorist base, or any other action. The team leader raises his hand issuing a predetermined signal, gets up, and starts walking. The team gets up as one united entity and follows him inland, into enemy territory.

Beyond the operational advantage of functioning as a combat team with stronger firepower and the ability to perform complicated military missions, it is also the convergence of personal talents into an entity that transforms it into a whole, greater than the sum of its parts.

For this to happen, a team has to be built on the personal ties and connections of its individual members. This will enhance the team's cohesion and spirit. The special energy derived from close-knit relationships evolves and enables the team energy to go kinetic, to fight and to win. Relationships matter in combat as much as if not more than they do in civilian life.

CHAPTER 7

Advanced Training

Combat Diving

Most people cannot begin to imagine what it means to be a Navy SEAL and may have in mind the enchanting images of the extraordinary explorations of Jacques-Yves Cousteau. In the 1940s, Cousteau, a French marine researcher, developed the first "self-contained underwater breathing apparatus" (known by its acronym SCUBA). The first SCUBA Cousteau used was a closed-system oxygen rebreather. Today's military diving equipment is based on Cousteau's model. This device is essentially an artificial lung connected to a small oxygen tank that divers attach to their bellies. Inside the lung, oxygen flows through a special compartment containing soda lime, which absorbs carbon dioxide (CO_2), a potentially toxic substance released from the diver's blood system when he exhales.

A short hose with a mouthpiece connects the diver to this closed-system breathing apparatus so that a small quantity of pure oxygen is breathed and rebreathed by the diver. The CO_2 is removed and, most important for Navy SEALs to ensure the stealth dive, no bubbles are released to the surface that would expose a diver's position. This is unlike recreational diving gear, in which bubbles exhaled from the diver's regulator emerge to the surface of the water.

Diving time with the closed system is up to three or four hours, much longer than with recreational diving equipment. The closed-circuit diving method demands strenuous training and high fitness. It requires a different way of breathing and may cause residual effects: headaches, rapid breathing, dizziness, and even loss of consciousness. Another common myth about combat diving is the question regarding the depth at which we dive. Most people are surprised and seem disappointed to learn that we normally dive no deeper than twenty feet. If we did dive deeper, the compressed oxygen would become toxic, causing sudden epileptic-like seizures and almost immediate loss of consciousness.

During the diving training phase in Atlit, which began in September 1986, we spent entire days and nights in and under the water. First, we learned the basics of oxygen rebreather diving in the warm Mediterranean waters. We learned how to assemble the gear, how the rebreather operates, and how to manage breathing with this challenging diving gear. Rebreather diving has to be learned, practiced, and mastered. You need to be able to control your breathing. Even while exerting yourself during an operational dive, you must control your breathing so as not to cause hyperventilation, the signs of which are headache, dizziness, and loss of consciousness.

As the dives became longer, we developed a physical situational awareness that actually helped control our breathing. Longer dives become possible once the breathing method is mastered and you regulate the amount of oxygen you use. If there is too much oxygen, the rebreather inflates and pulls the diver toward the surface. During an underwater demolition operation in enemy territory, you do not want to surface suddenly, for obvious reasons. Mastering the rebreather allows you to navigate and maneuver in shallow water without losing control over buoyancy.

I enjoyed this phase of the training. Reexperiencing the warm and cozy feeling of the Mediterranean waters felt like coming home, back into the natural habitat of my childhood and youth. It was familiar but also exciting and challenging at the same time.

Early mornings found us sitting in the briefing room in preparation for our upcoming dive. We reviewed various combat diving and demolition procedures and memorized safety and emergency drills. Again and again our trainers emphasized the balance we needed to maintain between following procedures, completing the mission, and safeguarding our own and our buddies' lives. Don't give up, we were told. You have to learn to stay underwater even when it seems impossible – but do not cross the point of no return.

With all this in mind, we would gear up and head off to sea. Our trainers and a medical rescue team in a Zodiac rubber boat would wait for us as we walked out in our gear toward the water. We jumped off the stony reef into the water pair by pair, connected to each other by a one-and-a-half-yard lifeline or "buddy line." This bond was always present. It was a physical bond and a bond of mutual responsibility connecting us. We would gather near the boat, sync our diving watches, get clearance, mutually signal the OK sign, let the air out of the buoyancy control vest, and then slip underneath the surface, turning upside down and swimming to a depth of fifteen feet in the direction the compass indicated.

Dive after dive, we endured endless hours submerged in seawater, breathing pure oxygen while dreaming about graduation and sabotaging enemy ships in hostile waters. We put a lot of effort into detaching ourselves from the hard and painful here and now in anticipation of reaching our goal: becoming Navy SEALs.

One early November morning, my buddy and I were diving in open water, heading out to sea. The water was getting colder as the days got shorter and the temperature outside dropped. The water of the eastern Mediterranean is not normally very clean and transparent, but that morning the water was crystal clear. While diving away from the coast, we saw the ground slowly drop away and through the lucid water, the surface seemed as if it was hanging above like a huge infinite ceiling. It felt like flying in a strange three-dimensional world. Weightless, fearless, and full of awe, I found it to be almost a religious experience. A school of barracuda fish swam past us. A giant sea turtle swam underneath. For about three hours, we navigated along a predetermined path.

About a mile offshore, the Zodiac rubber boat was waiting for us, secured in place by an anchor. I could see the outline of the rubber boat, its bow tied to a red buoy. The buoy was tied to a long cable that dropped vertically toward the deep Mediterranean floor. As we approached, still concentrating on my compass and depth gauge, I became aware of some huge, dark object lying on the seabed below. As we swam closer, the outlines of a sunken ship appeared and became clearer and clearer, its two masts rising, reaching just below the surface. Schools of fish were swimming around us. It was a breathtaking sight.

Back at the base, we rinsed our gear. During the debriefing, I thought about this dive and that the grandeur of those moments would probably never return. I was right. As the days passed and winter settled in, the water got colder day by day. Our dives in the open sea were relocated to the filthy waters of the port of Haifa. The sunny days were gone for now, turning into long, dark, wet, and cold nights. Dives got longer and more complicated, with additional operational protocols to be learned and carried out. More combat gear including limpet mines, combat diving vests with attached equipment, and weapons for attack and self-defense were added to our gear.

Operational briefing sessions were followed by individual prep work, studying maps and aerial photos of the training area, preparing the diving gear, and double-checking everything. Each diving pair would then discuss and metaphorically walk (or rather dive) through that night's dive plan, the idea being that both should know and plan for all the components of each phase of the dive in detail. We rehearsed demolition protocols and tried to anticipate what might go wrong – an unexpected sea current that might throw you off course, a target (ship) that might have moved – and what our reaction might be. These dry runs are central to the prep phase.

As I gained experience in operational procedures, I came to understand and appreciate all of the time devoted to prep and simulation. I understood that watching a presentation and listening to an oral briefing were not sufficient to be able to execute the complicated and challenging procedures we would be required to perform underwater. The way human memory works under stress (and underwater) is not the same as in everyday events. The brain's ability to retrieve the memory required to perform a task in a new or different setting is not as straightforward as one might think. The stress of being underwater and regulating your breathing while navigating in a harsh environment makes the implementation of learned protocols more difficult. That is why it is so important to learn, review, and drill the plan before diving. By internalizing all aspects of the planned dive and turning them into an internal conversation and by composing and memorizing a "dive story," one can focus and retrieve the necessary information intuitively. These methods ensure safe and successful operations.

Around midnight, we would suit up in our full diving gear and wetsuits. They're called wetsuits for two reasons. One is that the rubber is not totally sealed, so water penetrates the suit when the diver enters the water. It does, however, insulate the diver and sustain body temperature by minimizing water flow. And two, because the wetsuit was usually not dry from the previous night's dive. In any case, the process of stepping out of your warm clothes and donning a cold wetsuit and the rest of the diving gear was not fun. In the back of our minds was also the anticipation of facing the unknown.

We stood in formation and passed one last inspection by the instructors. It was now finally time to get wet. The sea felt cool as the water flowed up and down our spines. We shook off the chill and started swimming, our wetsuits warming slowly from the heat of our bodies.

Seaports are characterized by the singular activities within their confines. Ships tied to piers; cranes loading and unloading containers; harbor pilots and tugboats rushing to and fro. A unique smell, a mixture of diesel fuel, the salty sea breeze, and rotting sea algae hovers over the whole port. While awaiting clearance to start the dive, I would watch the large container ships and try to imagine where they had been and where they were going next, mentally taking me far away from the cold, miserable present.

Finally, the order to dive is given. Face mask donned, mouthpiece in place, checking the flow of oxygen and inhaling its slightly bitter, dry taste, we make sure the buddy line is connected between the two buddies' wrists. Then come the mutual signals of "OK," then "dive." These hand signals are exchanged above water. For the duration of the dive, all communication between us will be conducted by hand signals.

While emptying the air out of my buoyancy vest, I become heavier and begin to descend. All of a sudden there are no ships, no smells, and hardly any light. I sometimes hear the distant sounds of propellers, engines, and generators. Or I hear nothing at all but the subtle sound of my own breathing. I start swimming, moving my fins, checking the illuminated compass, depth gauge, and diving watch, concentrating on maintaining direction, depth, and speed. The darkness is interrupted only by occasional shades of gray, dim rays of light penetrating the dirty water from a nearby pier. As I approach a ship, I get the sense of being in its shadow as the darkness engulfs me. Sometimes I bump right into the huge steel hull of a ship. Under the stern, in complete darkness, the compass sometimes goes askew due to the deviation caused by the ship's magnetic field. Sometimes I get an uncanny feeling that I am diving in circles and have no idea which way is up or down. In such situations, one may lose the ability to recognize the direction of the dive, the intended direction that will lead me and my buddy, in an emergency, out from under the ship.

Vertigo is a well-documented phenomenon that affects fighter pilots and divers alike. When the sensory and vestibular inputs cannot be integrated by the brain, one loses balance and sense of direction and feels the world is spinning. While suffering vertigo underwater is usually not as dangerous as in the air, it can cause disorientation or even a panic attack. In extreme cases, vertigo can lead to a diver's death by causing him to descend into the depths instead of surfacing.

During long dives, I had to learn to circumvent my impaired eyesight and hearing. The human ears cannot register the direction of incoming sounds underwater. Even the sense of touch becomes dulled after hours in the cold water. I learned to depend on maximum alertness in order to recognize the slightest change in light which might indicate a nearby ship or pier. This heightened awareness, I knew, would enable me and my buddy to swim up to and parallel to the pier, as briefed.

During those long hours spent underwater, I learned about decision making and generating action with the little information I had at hand. Use whatever data you may have, rely on your training and your buddy, and make quick but calculated decisions. Be ready to acknowledge and correct any errors of judgment or action. Know the plan but be flexible enough to change it to accommodate a changing environment. The plan is important because it enables maximum preparedness. The plan guides you and sets the framework and boundaries of the operational mission. It also provides preplanned solutions to foreseeable problems and changes. But the sea, the enemy, or other circumstances can catch you off guard at any time. That's when flexibility is called for: the ability to think fast, change the plan if necessary, and improvise.

After hours of diving in the cold, dark water, the oxygen rebreather starts to work less efficiently, causing the level of CO_2 to rise and the diver's breathing to accelerate. At this point, the diver becomes fatigued due to both low body temperature and accelerated breathing. Breathing can become uncomfortable and even painful with the rebreather apparatus.

But you know you can't stop. You just can't. It's all about stamina. Determination. Endurance.

These are the core values of the Shayetet. Written in blood, as they say. This was the message in training: in every exercise, drill, or operation, one must endure and execute the mission. Every night, in the course of a structured ceremony, we would each report our mistakes and behavioral shortfalls. There was a price tag for each fault or failure. Many of our punishments were associated with lack of endurance. Punishments included a long run, swim, or dive. Minor infractions such as a microscopic freckle on your AK-47 would cost you a four- or five-mile run. A secondary infraction such as reporting late to training would cost you eight to ten miles. Major infractions meant you got your butt kicked straight home and out of training. Out of the unit.

When you ran, you had to touch a road sign or a specific tree at its midpoint and then head back to base. "All five fingers on target" – this expression is used in the Shayetet training to highlight the value of striving to fulfill the mission. It signifies the unwritten contract between the warrior and the unit and between the warrior and his own determination. Never give up or give yourself a break. Go all out.

Forty with Forty: The Maximum Operational Scenario

In order to get to this point and to develop endurance, we had to pass another maximum-scenario *masa*, combined with a combat diving operational exercise.

The forty with forty was a legendary operational attack scenario in which the Shayetet was to sink the ships anchored in an enemy harbor. Approaching by sea (using SEAL delivery boats) was not possible, so the plan was to stealthily walk through enemy territory, carrying all the combat diving gear, and advance as far as possible toward the harbor. Then the plan was to enter the water, swim the remaining distance, dive, and attack. This was an out-of-the-box operational solution that had turned into an attack plan. While it was never ultimately carried out, it was nevertheless incorporated into the Shayetet training course, perhaps as a rite of passage ritual.

After the long and strenuous training program to reach our physical capacity, and upon acquiring the necessary combat diving level, it was time to hit the road. It didn't seem real. A few hours before the *masa*, I prepared my gear. I assembled the oxygen rebreather and tested it. I prepared my raiding (infantry) vest and buoyancy control and then took care of the limpet mines. After securing my AK-47, commando knife, and flair gun, I stopped to make sure nothing was missing. Standing there with the rest of the team, I could read the expressions on their faces – like me, nobody was quite sure that we could actually do this. There was a disturbing silence. No one said a word. Everyone was busy getting their gear ready. Suddenly Gidi raised his head and said, "It's a piece of cake" and started laughing. And then "Let's go, lions!" he shouted, and we all joined in, firing each other up and motivating the team. At that moment, we all felt and believed that we could do it.

We each carried a massive amount of weight. This *masa* was (inaccurately) called forty with forty. Forty kilometers carrying forty kilograms. While the walking distance was more or less correct, about forty kilometers (twenty-five miles), the weight carried by each soldier was much more than forty kilograms (about ninety pounds). The combat diving gear alone weighed about ninety pounds, but the vest, AK-47, and five thirty-round magazines added about thirty-five pounds. For the smaller, skinnier guys, this was more than their total body weight. Then there was the swim and the attack dive. A good distance to go and about five hours in the water.

The diving gear was packed in huge duffle bags tied to special carrier-backpacks. They looked humongous. Each of us tied two short strings from the top of the carrier to a fifteen-inch stick. As we walked, we would push the stick up, about every two minutes, to bounce the bag and allow the blood to flow back into our arms. Every hour, we stopped for a drink and short rest, and the doctor would check us to make sure that no one's arms were going numb. For some of us, it felt pretty close, but in the context of this impossibly hard physical challenge, that seemed to be the last thing we had to worry about.

After running for hours, we reached the designated beach, quickly changing into wetsuits and diving gear and adjusting our oxygen rebreathers. Each soldier carried two limpet mines – explosive charges the size of a medium backpack with time mechanism detonators. After the hot, sweaty run, the cool water welcomed us, as we slipped into the sea and started swimming. The relief was short-lived. The swimming pace was fast, and it was hard to keep up with the team leader. To make matters worse, my leg muscles now started to spasm. The pain was unbearable. However, it had to be bearable, since there was no other option but to swim on. As we swam in the dark and my leg muscles warmed up, the swimming became just very hard, but far less painful. After about ninety minutes, we were closing in on the location of our attack site – a military naval compound that was guarded and well lit. Our mission was to stealthily penetrate the compound and sabotage the naval vessels in the harbor.

I opened the oxygen valve, put the mouthpiece in place, and donned my diving mask. The familiar taste of the oxygen filled my mouth. I turned to my buddy, we both signaled "OK." I looked at my compass, registered the right diving course, signaled "dive," and pressed the air release button on my buoyancy control vest. As we descended, we both turned upside down and started swimming, leveling at a depth of fifteen feet. I was shivering, not because the water was very cold. It wasn't. The feeling was one of exhaustion and the depletion of energy. With my battery running on low, all I could do was shiver. I navigated, using my compass, depth gauge, and dive watch, trying hard to keep my situational awareness intact. I was so tired. I could feel the blurring of my perception as we approached the naval compound.

Following the preplanned route, I found it harder and harder to stay awake. At a certain point, when I signaled "OK?" to my buddy, he did not respond. Turning swiftly around, alert that he might have lost consciousness, I realized that he was moving his fins, holding onto my weight belt, and swimming – but obviously fast asleep. When I gave him a friendly slap on his cheek, he woke up, startled. I asked again, "OK?" He confirmed and started laughing. Through the mouthpiece, he sounded like a sea lion, barking. With the rebreather's mouthpiece in my mouth, I smiled to myself, and we continued on.

The naval compound was well guarded, surrounded by underwater fences, a defense to keep enemy divers out. This time, we were playing the enemy. We found our way in and headed toward the ship that was marked as ours to attack. As we approached the pier, the water was shallow and filthy. The light from the strong projectors illuminated the compound and made the water look milky gray. It was hard to get oriented and to find the right ship. We were on course, at a depth of fifteen feet. Every few minutes, we passed under another narrow pier and the naval vessels that stood alongside. Suddenly my head banged into something hard, waking me up. I had bumped into one of the pier's pillars. This time I started laughing. I was commanding the dive pair and had briefly dozed off. I moved my shoulders, letting the cold water run into my wet suit, to refresh myself. I found it hard to remember the exact count of the piers we had already crossed and took a few seconds to reorient myself. We needed to find our target ship, which was located at a certain pier.

Once we got there, we attached the limpet mines to the hull of the target ship. Of course, these were only inert training mines. We had no intention of harming our own vessels. Once all four mines had been attached to the ship, we headed out of the compound, to the predetermined meeting point. When we reached it, we reported to our instructors, who were supervising our dive from a Zodiac rubber boat. We were ordered to wait. It was near the port breakwater in the shade of large stones, full of algae and filth. Another two pairs arrived with us, roughly at the same time. We had to wait for the other five pairs who were still diving in the compound. We filled our buoyancy control vests with air and floated near the rocks. In seconds, we were all sound asleep.

Sometime later, the instructors woke us up. "Dunk your heads in the water!" they shouted, as punishment for snatching those precious moments of sleep. The last pair finally arrived. It was time to start the long swim back.

I can't recall much from that swim. Every now and then, someone would swim away from the team, only to be woken up and pulled back by the others. It was around four in the morning when we finally hit the ground at the beach we had left five hours earlier. In the water, diving gear weighs nothing. It has to have neutral buoyancy. If it sinks or floats, you cannot maintain the depth of the dive. But when your feet hit the ground, and you start walking out of the water, the full weight of the gear becomes immense. By the time you step onto the shore, it feels like a ton. I walked out of the water, negotiating the transition from zero gravity to this ridiculous situation. Taking a step at a time, I regained my posture and moved toward the area where we then had to change back into our infantry outfits and prepare for the long run back to base.

Then moments of despair take effect. Total depletion. Exhaustion. "How can I keep on going?" I asked myself. "I cannot stop," I told myself. I knew.

Dan, two years my senior, was one of my instructors. We grew up together at Maagan Michael. In the Shayetet, he kept a safe distance, not to confuse me (and himself) regarding our roles. At home, over the weekends when I got liberty, we could interact and laugh at the bizarre situation.

Now I was standing there, unable to move. Feeling helpless, I was starting to sink into myself, to withdraw from what was happening around me. Dan looked at me. He realized something was wrong. He walked over, put his hand on my shoulder and said, "Come on, you can do it, pull yourself together, Yotam."

Dan was my instructor. He could be assertive; he had harassed me and the other guys many times during training. This time he sounded compassionate. It was as if he connected the cables from his battery to mine, charging me with energy and motivation. I shook myself, nodded in gratitude, put on my vest and the huge backpack, and, like an agitated turtle, started walking, then running to catch up with the team.

The Endurance versus Safety Conflict

A person's ability to endure, even in the most trying of circumstances, and to maintain physical and mental stamina are both imperative to succeed in completing training missions such as the forty with forty. But the fact is that after hours of diving in the cold and dark, continued operation becomes physically and mentally exhausting and can be dangerous – very dangerous, to both oneself and to one's diving buddies. These are the situations we prepare for in training.

Every year there were a number of diving accidents caused by this conflict: the need to persevere and operate in adverse circumstances versus the need to preserve one's safety. It is nearly impossible to define the exact point at which the diver feels he cannot continue the mission. This is not a theoretical question. If a diver loses consciousness underwater because he doesn't recognize that he has gone beyond his limits, he can be seriously hurt or even drown. The key to survival is knowing what we call the emergency rescue drill. This procedure is rehearsed at the beginning of every diving exercise. When a diver senses that his buddy is not reacting, it's up to him to get his partner afloat and to the surface quickly and to perform mouth-to-mouth resuscitation. Over the years, many events such as these ended well, but some ended tragically with the death of one or both divers.

CHAPTER 8

Going Operational

Getting Our Wings

In 1987, my team completed the grueling Shayetet training course. It was a dream come true for me and the conclusion of many extreme tests and challenging physical and psychological experiences. The final week of training was fun and empowering. In a series of rite of passage rituals, we officially became members of the Shayetet clan. The first stage was an unexpected *masa*. With our backpacks full of sand, we ran a short distance, climbing to the top of the tall water tower on our base. There, one after the other, we opened our backpacks, drew out our commando knives, and stabbed the sand-filled plastic bottles, allowing the sand to pour out for good. Those same backpacks, notoriously used in the *masa'ot* and also carried during punishments and those extra mile runs at nights, symbolized the hard coin payment for offenses we had committed. Now we had the great feeling of relief just knowing that those days were over.

In the second stage, we received new shoes and uniforms. We didn't have to be dressed like trainees anymore. The worn-out, gun oil–stained fatigues were gone, and we had new, much better-looking uniforms. According to the summer dress code, Shayetet warriors were allowed to wear a military button-down shirt, short military trousers, and sandals.

There was only one thing still missing: the Shayetet insignia – the bat wings. We knew we would receive them before the commencement ceremony. We would pin the bat wings onto our uniform shirts at chest level and cover them with tape, to be exposed at the commencement ceremony. We had heard about past rituals in which the bat wings were issued underwater. In the ancient Crusader castle on the Shayetet base, there was a small, deep bay where those dives were routinely conducted. A table and two chairs were placed on the seabed. The team leader and one more instructor would sit there in full diving gear, at a depth of fifteen feet. Pair by pair, the graduating warriors would dive toward the table and receive their shiny new bat wings.

On the evening before the commencement ceremony, a storm broke out, with the accompanying strong winds and high waves. The dive had to be cancelled. We celebrated over dinner at a local restaurant. We had a great time, a few good laughs, and forgot about the disappointment of the cancelled dive. When it was time for dessert, Yonat stepped out of the restaurant's kitchen with a big cake.

Yonat grew up on Kibbutz Maagan Michael, the youngest daughter of Yossele Dror, the legendary founder of the Shayetet. She served her military term in the Shayetet as our team's admin. She proved to be much more than an admin. With her smile, care, and compassion, she kept us motivated. Most of the guys were totally in love with her. For me, she was (and still is) like a sister. We had grown up together on the kibbutz.

The cake was rich and creamy and delicious. As we were eating, a sudden silence fell over the soldiers as they discovered the big surprise – the bat wings were hidden inside our pieces of cake.

The Warriors Squadron
After commencement, our team moved to the Operational (or Warriors) Squadron. This was the beginning of our operational tenure. During my first few months in the Warriors Squadron, I served in the fast assault and delivery boats unit, a subunit of the Shayetet. Some of the guys had medical issues and could not dive. It was decided that half of the team would be assigned to operating the boats. While I was still in good diving condition, I was assigned to that unit. Handling the RIBs (rigid inflatable boats, a better version of the Zodiac rubber boats) and the larger cigar-shaped boats was enjoyable, and I was able to draw on my previous nautical experience. I had a lot of sea time on sailboats during my childhood on the kibbutz, so adapting to the strong motor vessels was rather easy. Training continued as we learned and mastered new procedures. And then, of course, there was the operational work.

Most of the operations of the Shayetet remain under wraps for many years. Some, however, reach the headlines. Shayetet operations make the headlines in one of the following cases: (1) the operation was a resounding success; (2) the operation was a dramatic failure; or (3) the operation is used as a show of power to gain political or diplomatic advantage. Sometimes, getting a message to your enemy necessitates the projection of power. The media serves as a sounding board to amplify these messages.

In the summer of 1987, we had intel that an armed Lebanese militia was contemplating an attack on northern Israel. We were sent in to disrupt their plans. Near their military compound in the south of Lebanon, they deployed armed patrol trucks with heavy machine guns. At night, they would drive up and down the Lebanese Coastal road and occasionally would open fire at anything that looked suspicious at sea. They had previous experience of being attacked so were on high alert. The objective of the attack was to keep the terrorists on the defensive so that they would be unable to go on the offensive, to attack. In order to convey this message, our attack had to be painful.

I sat with the team in the briefing room while the head of the Shayetet was giving the final instructions. Eager to go and get this operation underway, I thought for a minute about what we were going to do. My team would man the SEAL delivery boats. We would sneak into the Lebanese coastal waters and deliver the raiding strike force close enough so that they would be able to swim ashore. We would wait at sea, at a reasonable distance, and upon receiving a signal, we would return toward the beach to pick up our soldiers once they had completed the mission. We knew that it was highly likely that the pickup phase would follow an engagement with the enemy and would take place under fire. When you are twenty years old and eager to perform, you do not let such thoughts take hold of you. This is what we had signed up for.

The RIB has a powerful jet thruster and an internal diesel engine. Its inflated sides stand very low above the waterline, making it perfect for stealth operations. It has excellent maneuvering ability and can carry six to eight raiders in full combat gear.

The raiding force consisted of two teams, about twenty-five warriors. This necessitated the use of four RIBs and two larger cigar boats, one of them serving as the command post for the operation. Just before dusk, the SEAL delivery boats converged behind the stern of a missile boat – a much larger naval vessel that would serve as backup and provide remote firepower. If things went wrong, they could fire cannons and shell the beaches to assist us.

Maintaining complete radio silence, the missile boat headed toward the designated landing beach, with our small flotilla following behind. When the missile boat blew its horn and took a sharp turn to the right, we continued, heading straight ahead on the course that the missile boat and our compasses indicated. We were still far from land, and it would take time until we would be able to see the lights of the Lebanese beaches.

The command cigar boat was surrounded by the four RIBs, cruising in tight formation. I was driving the second RIB on the left side. The second cigar boat stayed behind, as backup.

In the twilight, I could see Captain Uri Teitz, the commanding officer of the Shayetet, standing in the command vessel's cockpit. Only a few months earlier, he'd shaken my hand on commencement day after the IDF chief of staff exposed my bat wings. Since then I had started to become familiar with him, mostly during briefings or formal talks. As a young warrior, I did not interact with him on a regular basis.

The sea was fairly calm. The boats slowed down as we neared the coast. A hand signal was given, and the raiders put on their gear: vest, buoyancy belt, AK-47 and additional team weapons, PK machine guns, LAW anti-tank missiles and RPGs. They painted their faces with dark paste. It was a moonless night, and they were hardly noticeable on the RIBs. I found it hard to recognize the faces of my friends and former instructors. They had transformed into a ghostly stealth strike force.

Concentrating on my steering, I kept a close but safe distance from the other boats. I kept an eye on the dashboard, checking the illuminated gauges which showed that the boat was operating well, noting engine heat, oil pressure, and battery charging level. As we approached, the illuminated coast became visible. I could sense and smell the presence of nearby land.

The command boat stopped, as did the rest of the boats. The raiders put on fins over their boots, and with their gear, slipped off my RIB into the water. They swam swiftly into formation, joining the other team, and started swimming toward the beach. Using night-vision gear, we followed their stealth approach. Once a beachhead was formed, the teams walked silently out of the water and prepared for their mission. Each team walked a short distance to predetermined spots and set up an ambush along the coastal road. The ambush sites on the coastal road were set up about a mile apart. The plan was that when an armed patrol truck passed one team, it would be identified and marked as a legitimate enemy target. Then the second team would be alerted and attack it.

After about an hour, we heard the radio communication between the teams. "Take it. It's yours," we heard. Two minutes later, an explosion lit the dark sky. An RPG was fired by one of the warriors, who jumped into the road and hit the truck between its headlights, stopping the truck. A second explosion followed, flipping the truck over and hitting its passengers. The team then opened fire with their PKs and AK-47s. Two hand grenades were thrown toward the remains of the truck. The terrorists didn't have a chance. A few minutes later, two more armed pickup trucks rushed to the scene. They met the same fate as the first one.

Having fulfilled the mission, the teams were ready to withdraw. They walked swiftly to the landing beach, and after a short prep to get their gear into swimming mode, they swam away from the shore. At this stage in the retreat, the raiders were highly vulnerable. They swam at a relatively slow pace to get away from the beach without being discovered. This is when we moved in to evacuate them.

On the beach, we saw that armed enemy troops and vehicles had gathered. They began to open fire at us. We were on our way, a few hundred yards from the beach, slowly approaching the teams in the water. Shells and bullets whistled past us, some just over my boat and others hitting the water not far from the inflated sides of the RIB. I braced as much as possible, hoping to escape the bullets flying nearby, leaving red tracks of light in the dark night sky. I pushed the throttle forward, gaining speed as I approached the swimming team. They quickly climbed onto the boat and remained very low, taking cover close to the deck. I was the only one sitting vertically in the driver's seat, trying to minimize my presence as a potential target. When all were aboard, I turned the boat away from the beach and slowly accelerated. Pushing the throttle too hard would create white foam behind the stern of the boat, giving away our position. I had no intention of becoming an easy target for the enemy. In a few minutes, we had made it safely beyond the enemy's range of fire.

Mission accomplished, we now headed back to base, arriving before dawn.

The boats were lifted out of the water by a crane, and on the pier, we were greeted by the technical teams who were there to take care of the boats. After washing our gear, making sure all was in place, we ate a light meal, and then it was time to get some sleep.

At around noon, we gathered in the briefing room. It was time to debrief the operation. Spirits were high as we waited for the session to start. Captain

Uri Teitz was never late for a meeting or any scheduled event. It was odd that his chair in the front row remained empty. After long minutes, we heard a commotion from outside. Something was happening on the beach or in the bay. We ran outside to see what was happening and to help. One of the teams in BUD/S training was operating a RIBs in the bay. They spotted a man lying unconscious in the water. They lifted him onto the boat and began CPR on the unconscious man. It turned out to be Captain Uri Teitz, head of Shayetet 13. Uri was a healthy and fit thirty-eight-year-old warrior. After the long and stressful night, he had decided to work out and ran for a few miles. Then he entered the sea to swim across the bay. It is believed that he suffered cardiac arrest. We lost him.

It was a blow. It was hard to believe that this could happen to Uri. To our commanding officer. We were in shock, and the grief was unbearable. It took some time for the unit to bounce back from this loss. The loss of leadership is a challenge in ways that, at the time, I could not fully internalize.

The operation had been a success, and the message had gotten across to the enemy, but for the Shayetet, the outcome was tragic. This was one example when the Shayetet, unwillingly, made it into the media.

In the months that followed, I started feeling that I wasn't where I should or wanted to be. I really wanted to dive. To be a combat diver. It wasn't a trivial move. Most warriors who transfer from one squad (or subunit) to another move from the divers' squad to the boat squad. The reason is usually loss of diving ability due to health issues. I wanted to dive and started working on this, trying to sway my commanders. After I had received a few negative answers, one of the designated divers was wounded in training. All of a sudden, I was now the answer to solving the problem, and my wish to become a diver became a reality. I joined the Underwater Demolition Team.

CHAPTER 9

The Journey to Leadership

An Uncertain Candidate

I loved operational diving. It suited me perfectly. I learned fast, acquired good operational understanding, and most of all, I felt like a fish in the water. But being a good diver and a good warrior is not enough. Even operating with an exceptional team of soldiers is not enough. Operational missions are complicated and dangerous and demand thorough planning, precise coordination, and a figure who will energize, inspire, and lead the warriors to operational success. While operational planning is spearheaded by the Shayetet commanders at headquarters, it is up to the team commander in the field to connect the dots, to oversee tactical training and operational readiness, to plan and manage the team's tight schedule, and to sustain the morale and positive energy of the team. The team commander leads his men to battle and has a key role to play in special operations units.

Years later, as the unit's psychologist, I played a central role on the committee that selected candidates for team leadership. In the Shayetet, as in most other IDF units, officers begin their careers as enlisted men and women. After the initial year's service, some are chosen to be sent to officers' training school. These candidates would become the next generation of combat team leaders. I interviewed each candidate, assessing his motivation, emotional maturity, and cognitive abilities, as well as his current operational status. At the end of the process, I presented a review of each candidate to the committee with my prediction regarding his chances of success. After long discussions – sometimes heated debates – the Shayetet commanding officer would make the final decision.

There were always multiple candidates for each vacant leadership spot. Sometimes, however, the best candidates, the natural leaders, the aces among the team were reluctant to extend their contracts and take on this challenge. Shayetet warriors serve an additional eighteen months beyond what was at the time a mandatory three-year service (today the regular mandatory service for men has been reduced, although special forces serve longer). Team leaders are required to serve an additional year, for a total of five and a half years.

Some candidates had already made their plans for the future: enroll in college, start a business, travel abroad. Some were just not willing to make the commitment. The interviews with these reluctant candidates became motivational talks in which I would share my own story and experiences. My arguments of persuasion included the prospective benefits one could expect on a personal level, including self-fulfillment. The interviews with these tough cases usually turned out to be the most interesting and meaningful. They were not merely job interviews, nor were they recruitment meetings. They were intimate conversations meant to guide these young SEALs in making a major career decision. It was understood that choosing this option to join the Shayetet chain of command would likely determine a young man's commitment to a long military career. A life-changing decision.

In the winter of 1988, I was one of those candidates. Eager to meet the challenge, I was a bit uncertain, but nevertheless fueled and motivated to become a team leader.

A few months after graduating the SEAL training course, we were presented with the scenario of a mission gone wrong. As opposed to routine operational exercises in which all measures for success are taken into consideration, this exercise focused on managing mission failure. We would have to face a situation in which we were exposed and would have to retreat without completing the mission and without being able to meet up with the delivery boats. The challenge was to survive unnoticed in enemy territory. In the briefing room, I skimmed the handwritten briefings posted on the wall and reviewed the mission, objectives, and battle plan. I was eager to know who my diving buddy would be. At that stage, I was usually appointed to lead a diving pair but was surprised when I saw my name on the board as diver number two, pairing with Lieutenant Commander Ronen, head of the Shayetet Underwater Demolition Unit. Ronen's participation in this exercise with me as his number two could not have been a coincidence. I presumed that it was connected to the fact that I, myself, was a candidate to be team leader.

The first phase of the exercise was briefed thoroughly. It was a complicated dive, with reconnaissance and attack missions combined. According to procedure, at a certain point during the dive, we were to stop for a safety report at the Zodiac boat. There we would be given a modification to the original operational script: the delivery boats were ordered to leave the area on the grounds that we were being tracked by the enemy. The hunter was now the potential prey. It was a long night, followed by a long day and then another long night until we finally made it back to base.

This is, in essence, a scenario which is considered to be mission failure and compels the transition to survival and escape mode. It demands a different set of operational dos and don'ts as well as a change in perception. We had been trained to initiate and take the offensive, but now we found ourselves vulnerable, tired, and alone. This situation elicits an entirely different psychological state. Facing mission failure and the fear of being captured, tortured, or killed is a lot to cope with and difficult to simulate.

After managing to get safely out of the danger zone, we took shelter in a deep cave that opened out to the sea and was hardly noticeable from land. We thought we would be able to stay there unnoticed until the search and rescue task force arrived. During those long hours of waiting, Ronen and I talked. Whispering, so that the sound of the sea would cover our presence, he asked me about my plans for the future. Since I had anticipated this conversation, I was ready with my response: "Yes. I do wish to become an officer and to lead my own team." And so the decision was made, and I began my journey to becoming an operational commander.

The Officers' Course

The same amphibian warrior training logic is also applicable to the Shayetet officers' course.

The first stage in the course is training to be an infantry platoon commander. On a hot summer's day, exactly three years into my military service, when most of the guys who had enlisted with me had taken off their uniforms and were discharged from the army, I reported to the officers' course. The officers' training base is located on high ground in the Negev Desert. I had already been an operational SEAL for sixteen months; going back to formal training with its accompanying harsh discipline was not easy. To make matters worse, during the weekend leave before the start of the course, Iris and

I had had a serious lovers' quarrel. The next morning I got up very early, got dressed in my uniform, and headed toward this new phase in my military career with a huge lump in my throat, anxious about our relationship.

With no phone or any other means of communications (cell phones and the internet did not exist back then), we both had time to reflect upon our relationship before our next meeting in a few weeks' time. We both knew that we had to sort out our intense emotions and to agree on just where our relationship was headed. In the meantime, I had to find a way to harness my internal motivation and assume the role of cadet. It was customary for experienced (and relatively older) special ops cadets to be granted some privileges in training. I did not need any discounts that would make my officers' course life easier. On the contrary. I realized that I needed to work hard and keep at bay the distractions in my mind (and in my aching heart) of home and Iris.

On the second day of the eight-month course, I approached my trainer, a young paratrooper who was my platoon commander. Weapons were then being assigned to us cadets. Soldiers, especially trainees, tend to avoid volunteering for extra work. Like a pack of lions, they can fight and kick ass, but as soon as this is over, the primary inclination is to rest and digest. I nodded and asked him, "Can I be assigned the MAG machine gun?" With a big smile, he nodded, and the deal was done. Just as in BUD/S training, handling the MAG in the officers' course meant working the hardest. With this move, I had caught the attention of my younger, new team members from various infantry brigades, and they looked at me with astonishment and respect. Sometimes breaking the (unwritten) rules can be most effective.

In the months that followed, we matured as platoon commanders. We learned the art and craft of mission command, to see the bigger picture of the battlefield. Deep inside, I had the feeling that I was wasting my time. I knew that I was going back to the Shayetet to lead my underwater demolition team. I did not think infantry and ground warfare would be my main focus once I was back at the Shayetet. To keep my spirits high, I gave my MAG a deep look several times a day, reminding myself that I must work hard and excel at everything they threw my way, regardless of what was to come later. In the months that followed, we were immersed in ground warfare, long night walks, navigating the desert terrain, leadership and command exercises, and much more. As our course was nearing its end, I felt an additional layer of maturity and realized that my command toolbox had grown. These new skills would serve me well when I got back to my team at the Shayetet.

I graduated the infantry officers' course with distinction and was invited for an interview by the head of the officers' school. It was a formal talk, and there was an exchange of niceties. When the colonel, an experienced paratrooper, asked me for my feedback about the course curriculum, I thought for a minute and replied, "Sir, there are two things that I feel need to be reviewed and perhaps changed." I took a deep breath and continued. "Most important, I believe that training safety standards are not up to par, here in officers' school." This was harsh criticism, but I felt that I had to convey my impression. We had too many close calls, and they were all related to an atmosphere of cutting corners and lack of discipline. A lethal training accident seemed to be just a short way off. The colonel did not move a muscle in his face.

"The second thing that comes to mind," I continued, "is totally different. We have learned to command, to give orders, and to lead our men into combat. While I will be going back to Shayetet 13, where most of the warriors are highly motivated, some of my co-trainees will be going back to the infantry brigades. These brigades are made up of soldiers who come from a variety of social and economic backgrounds. Some may wrestle with low motivation." I thought for another second, and even though I did not have the slightest clue that I would one day be a psychologist, I said, "I believe young platoon leaders need to get some training, some tools for working with these soldiers, how to detect troubling issues among the soldiers and intervene if soldiers show signs of distress."

Sadly, about two weeks after the end of our course, a cadet was killed during an urban warfare exercise. It was a totally avoidable death. I nearly screamed when I heard about the accident. I felt helpless and sad. The writing had been on the wall. About a decade later, when I became a certified clinical psychologist and again returned to the Shayetet, I was called upon to provide a workshop for officer course cadets on how to identify and deal with soldiers showing distress. It was satisfying for me that the observation I had made ten years earlier was now being applied and the importance to train officers in these skills recognized.

The next stage of the Shayetet officers course was training to be a naval officer. Until then I had had experience with short deployments aboard missile ships, patrol boats, and submarines. Some of our SEAL delivery vehicles were carried aboard these larger vessels. The idea behind this stage of training was to enhance a deeper understanding of naval warfare and to learn how larger ships are commanded. Naval officers think and operate very differently from infantry platoon leaders. The navy has its own specific culture and language, and even though the Shayetet is part of the navy, it too has its own special-forces ground warfare culture.

The last phase of the Shayetet officers' training consists of a unique course for Shayetet team leaders to educate and empower the young team leaders before they take on their new roles. We became familiar with the procedures of headquarters, the planning of operations, and then integrating all of this with what we had already learned during the previous stages of training. All of these elements in our training would become integrated and prove invaluable to Shayetet operational efforts.

Upon completion of this year-long training, a Shayetet warrior was now qualified to serve as a naval special warfare team leader.

CHAPTER 10

At the Helm

Team Leadership

In mid-1989, I returned to the Atlit Naval Base and was assigned command of the same underwater demolition team in which I had served only a year before. Commanding my peers, who by then had gained valuable experience, was challenging. It took me a few weeks to settle into my new position as team leader and to negotiate my place in the unit's echelon of command. It was also a challenge to find the balance between my new role as commander and the old camaraderie with my team.

One summer morning, as we were catching our breath after a long physical training (PT) session, Shay, Ronen's successor as the commander of the Shayetet's diving unit, called me over and said, "Something's cooking... Lebanese boats are preparing to launch an attack soon. We're going to stop them. Meet me in the office."

The underwater demolition operation described in the prologue of this book was not supposed to have been mine. There were older, more seasoned team leaders in our unit. It was a matter of sheer luck. Two officers were abroad, another had a health issue. Timing is everything.

I quickly entered battle procedure mode as we started preparations for this diving operation. First we secured the intel and learned the plans of the harbor. Then we prepared the gear, planned the dive, and conducted training dives and model operational exercises. By the time we were ready to go, I was tired and stressed. Long days of briefings, long nights of exercises – we were preparing for the real thing. While Shay, head of the divers' squad, was overseeing the whole operation, I was the one who ran the logistics, briefings, and coordination of all the pieces of the operational puzzle.

On the day of the operation, a few hours before we were supposed to board the SEAL delivery boats on our way north to Lebanon, we had our final briefing. In the front row of the small briefing room sat Admiral Ami Ayalon, deputy head of the Israeli Navy. Such operations were always briefed in the presence of the highest echelon of command for fine-tuning. Ami Ayalon was a former commander of the Shayetet and a highly decorated warrior. His determination and courage were second only to his leadership qualities. To me, he was (and still is) an inspiring role model.

The head of the delivery boat unit made his presentation, describing the course the assault divers (us) must take in order to get close enough to our target. He also noted the readiness of the delivery boat team to assist us if something were to go wrong. Then it was our turn. Shay, the operational diving team commander, stood near the podium and briefed the planned dive. Plan A, plan B, and plan C were introduced to spell out the various scenarios, backup plans, means of communications, and the available solutions to potential problems. I was sitting a few rows back, listening and slowly becoming more and more stressed out.

When it was my turn to speak, I got up, took a deep breath, walked up to the podium, and looked directly at Admiral Ayalon. I said, "Good morning, sir, my name is Yotam Dagan. I am the head of the operational diving team. I will be the commander of diving pair number 2." My heart was pounding, I was sweating, but as I started to walk (or rather dive) through my attack plan, I managed to pull myself together, calm down, and sharpen my thinking.

"After penetrating the harbor, I will find a place to take a peek above water without being seen." I pointed to the large aerial photo tacked onto the board. "Then I will identify my target boat, check the diving compass course, and attack the target." The admiral got up from his chair and walked up to me, at the podium. Ayalon was a very short, bald man with fierce blue eyes that projected charisma and a sense of power. It was probably the first time I really looked up to someone who was, in fact, much shorter than I was.

Ayalon pointed at the planned diving course and asked, "What is the depth of the water in this part of the harbor?"

"Intel says it's around five feet deep," I replied.

"And is that okay with you to dive at five feet, stealthily, and to get the job done?" he asked. While I was formulating my answer, he asked, "How shallow can you get and still get the job done?"

Before I opened my mouth to speak, I calculated: with the rebreather on my stomach, the limpet mines on my back, and me in the middle, that would be close to two and a half feet. I knew I needed at least four feet of water to maintain cover. As I was about to speak, an argument broke out in the room. Various numbers, depths, and constraints were thrown into the air by senior officers. I felt a sense of relief knowing that I didn't have to be the one to give the wrong answer. "I will make the final decision," Ayalon said, and nodded to me to continue my briefing.

A few minutes later, Ayalon returned to the podium, stared deeply into my eyes, and said, "Yotam – from under the neon lights in this briefing room, you have carte blanche to fulfill your mission, down to a depth of five feet. Chances are that you will need to go shallower. Being there, on your own, you will be aware of the illumination, the visibility of the water, and the presence of the enemy. This is your call – a command decision that you and only you can take. Be accountable and responsible for what you decide." I sat there, feeling how this short giant of a man had literally made me feel as if I had grown an inch taller, in that instant in which he empowered me.

Hours later, we packed and secured our combat gear onto the boats. It was customary for the Shayetet's command to accompany us to the pier, make last-minute decisions (when needed), and wish us good luck and farewell.

We boarded the long, cigar-shaped SEAL delivery boats. "They will call us back, before we do it," I thought to myself, knowing that this sometimes happens. An incoming piece of intel, some geopolitical change, disagreements among generals or politicians – any of these might justify the cancellation of the planned attack. But they didn't call us back. The boats sailed out of Atlit Bay, heading west, out to sea. A naval missile ship awaited us and escorted our small flotilla all the way to a designated point at sea, west of our target destination. Against the strong northern wind, the boats tossed and wrestled in the waves.

Ran, my number two and good friend, and I were sitting on chairs in the back, waiting for the distance to be covered, eager to get off the boat and to start the diving attack phase. I rehearsed our dive plan in my mind but ruminated, allowing my thoughts to wander just a little bit. Before dusk, the wind died down, and the sea became flat and calm. The boats stopped, and we waited for complete darkness to serve as our cover. Lowering the engines' exhausts into the water, to avoid any sound, we slowly penetrated the radar-guarded Lebanese shore. The missile ship stayed behind, ready to move in and back us up with its cannons and missiles if needed. As we approached, the lights of the harbor became visible. We stopped to take a look and see what was going on in the enemy's compound. There was a lot of traffic: people were walking, and cars were moving along the piers.

At the designated time, a signal was given, and each diver opened his bag, took out his combat gear, and got ready. As I was putting on my gear, my thoughts became clear, focused on the attack. I could almost visualize how I was entering a state of psychological tunnel vision. I pushed aside any irrelevant thoughts or distractions. I was in my element. We quickly but thoroughly checked each other to make sure that the oxygen rebreathers were in working order, the diving vests and buoyancy controls were in place, the limpet mines were safely attached to their carriers, and that our fins were ready. Then I painted my face with a dark makeup paste so that it would be harder to see me when I surfaced to take that peek, raising my head above water. I was ready to go.

When the command was given, Ran and I slipped into the water and swam toward the bow – the front of the boat. Shay and Eran were waiting for us. We quickly rechecked to make sure that all the gear was in working order and started swimming toward the harbor. We made sure that no Lebanese fishing boat was approaching, an event that would necessitate an emergency dive. We then swam to the point that was close enough for us to start our long and dangerous attack dive.

Shay gave us the "OK –go!" sign and we returned the sign to Shay and Eran. Ran and I turned to each other, connected our oxygen rebreathers, let the air out of the buoyancy control vests, and sank into the deep, dark water. On our own underwater, we undertook this important mission of deterring another deadly terrorist attack against Israel, against our homes and families, possibly against my kibbutz. Thinking back on being the eleven-year-old survivor of the 1978 coastal road terrorist attack, I invested great meaning in this mission. When the target boats exploded a few hours later, another circle of destiny became a reality. I had become a Navy SEAL team leader and accomplished my mission, sensing a feeling of closure.

The ride back to base was eventless and fast. I sat in the back of the boat feeling the adrenaline slowly draining from my body as a great fatigue came over me. It was a great feeling – I could now let go and savor the moment. At first light, the three long, green cigar SEAL delivery boats entered the Atlit Bay. The boats were lifted out of the sea onto the pier by a crane. We got off the boats and walked toward the barracks. After taking care of the combat gear, enjoying a warm shower, a light meal, and a little small talk, I got into bed and immediately fell asleep. Those had been very intense and stressful days, and I needed to rest.

Sometime in the afternoon I woke up, slowly opening my eyes, trying to determine where I was, what day it was, and what the new day would bring. Then came the physical sensations and vivid memories from last night's attack dive. It could have been a dream, but in fact, it was very real. Ran and I shared a small room. Officers were usually housed in rooms one story above the Shayetet barracks, but I chose to remain on the main level, with my team.

Ran was sitting on his bed, dressed in his uniform, so I guessed that he had been awake for some time and perhaps had had a chance to receive an update on the outcome of the operation. I slowly sat up in my bed, yawning. For five or six seconds, we looked at one another in silence. Then I smiled and asked, "*Nu..?*" (This is an untranslatable Yiddish word adopted into Hebrew that serves as a prompt, meaning something approximately like "So?")

"The boats were blown up. The planned enemy attack has been thwarted," Ran said with satisfaction.

After this operation and with more experience and a tonnage of sunken enemy boats under my belt, I finally positioned myself as commander and started thinking about my long-term goals for the team. Most of these goals had to do with operational preparedness and with doing it "my way," which meant strengthening the team's cohesion under my leadership.

With the authority of the role of commander also comes enormous responsibility: responsibility for the fulfillment of operational missions, ensuring a high level of professionalism, and perhaps most of all, the responsibility for the lives of my soldiers, of my team members. During my tenure, we returned to hostile waters and to land operations, carrying out complicated missions. We executed stealth operations under the radar without leaving a trace. We attacked when operations were deemed necessary, leaving sunken ships behind. We captured and hit terrorists in their bases, homes, and when they were on the run. Leading an operational SEAL team was perhaps the most challenging and rewarding role of any that I have filled.

The Search for Clarity

During this period, I was mostly stationed in the Warriors Squadron, the operational body of the Shayetet. Toward the end of my tenure, I also spent a few months at the SEAL training school, nurturing the next generation of warriors, some of whom would later join my team. It was during this phase that I faced, head on, the tragic results of a diving training exercise: the death of one of my men and the life-threatening wounds suffered by another.

The accident was horrific, so much so that I was unable to talk about it. It was too devastating. Feelings of guilt flooded over me for not being able to prevent it. After eighteen months as team commander, I felt that I needed some time and distance to work things through, even though I should have been up for a promotion. And so in the summer of 1990, I handed over the team to my successor. After five and a half years, I decided to leave military service.

It was a time of great confusion. I felt adrift, distressed. In an attempt to run away from the emotions surrounding the outcome of the tragic accident, I took a security job abroad, on an Italian pleasure liner. I also took a job in underwater construction, trying to find my calling.

In January 1991, I was called back to the Shayetet.

The first Gulf War was about to begin, and I was called up for reserve duty and was reappointed commander of my former team. For the next few weeks, we prepared for a mission which, in the end, did not transpire. As Iraqi Scud missiles hit Israel, we were there, preparing, briefing, and awaiting the green light. Sometimes, someone high in the C-suites steps on the brakes. For me, feeling the adrenaline rush once again, getting back into my former shoes (and fins), and stepping into operational command felt right. It was the right time for me to return to the Shayetet and give it another shot. I was assigned to the position of chief instructor and deputy head of the SEAL training school.

I was back.

The winter of 1991–92 was one of the stormiest in decades, and the Mediterranean waters were unseasonably cold. Training continued as usual, and there were a few close calls. Within the span of just a few weeks, three trainees had lost consciousness during oxygen rebreather exercises. I had been in my new position as chief instructor and deputy head of the SEAL school for only a few months and found these mishaps extremely worrisome. I felt that our share of good luck was running out. Let's face it, when you operate on the edge, luck becomes part of the equation. The trainees who had passed out were the leaders in their class, the most capable and talented.

Having experienced first-hand the catastrophic results of a training accident, I came to realize that there was something amiss in our safety procedures. Something was not working right in what sociologists call the "organizational culture."

Being a Navy SEAL meant putting your life on the line every day. It seemed obvious to me that in training, safety should always come first. But was I sure about this? How clear was it to us back then? While strict safety procedures were implemented during weapons and diving exercises, the need to simulate real-life conditions and to experience operational problem solving and decision making were crucial. Under these adverse conditions, the diver must utilize every ounce of learned knowledge, instinctive reactions, and motivation in order to endure. This creates a tension between safety (staying alive) and fulfilling the mission. This is especially true in the face of a full-scale war, in which plans would have to be formulated and targets marked. We knew that when the time came, we would be called upon to deliver.

A Lifeline

It was during one of the preps for a dangerous dive I had authorized that it suddenly clicked. I remember sitting in my office, the huge window facing the beautiful Atlit Bay behind me. On the desk in front of me were a British maritime admiralty map, an aerial photo, and the training file with the details of the upcoming training exercise. Two young officers, team leaders in training, presented the plans for tonight's dive. Every training exercise, whether a simple PT, a counterterror drill, or a complicated dive, was planned in detail and presented to the appropriate echelon of command for approval. The objective of this presentation was to ensure that all safety precautions were met and that the highest professional standards were applied.

The exercise they presented was for a long, complicated dive that was to be the final drill of the SEALs training. The team leaders were tired and wanted to get the presentation ritual behind them. Having been in their shoes not long before, I could empathize with their urge to get back to the teams, to oversee the diving gear checkup and begin the preparations for the upcoming dive. They too were waiting impatiently for their teams' graduation and for their new operational combat term to begin.

It was my task to make sure nobody would get hurt during the exercise. I thought hard, trying to visualize what I might be missing. I felt the stress of the enormous responsibility on my shoulders. I was the gatekeeper, the one whose job it was to oversee this training exercise. In this case, I felt that the stress and responsibility helped me to focus on the small details, but I was also aware that this kind of focus, under extreme duress, might disrupt my ability to think out of the box and miss things that might be right in front of me.

The diving drill for that night was categorized as a "maximum scenario." This meant that the operational plan must encompass all of the details and existing resources, including the distance to the target, the time needed to complete the drill, the oxygen rebreather capacity, and the soldiers' ability to call upon all their reserves (physical, mental, and emotional) to fulfill the task.

I was thinking about the last phase of the dive when the oxygen rebreathers are less effective and a high level of CO_2 might affect the divers' performance. This might lead to accelerated, shallow breathing, headaches, and possibly loss of consciousness.

"When you brief the soldiers on this last phase, how do you advise them when to abort the dive should it become too risky to continue? What criteria should be considered by the diver in order for him to make the decision to halt the exercise?" I asked. They both hesitated. They knew that there was no simple answer to this question. The conflict between the personal safety of the divers versus the value of mission fulfillment was self-evident, but were the divers trained well enough to recognize the blurry line that divided the two? They could not allow themselves to cross that line. The consequences could be life threatening.

Values or moral standards are the building blocks of high achievement. They are the pillars of integrity, the north star that helps navigate through a sea of mediocrity, negligence, and corruption. Values generate norms of behavior and the measurable, defined dos and don'ts that characterize every Navy SEAL's inner compass. But values are often put to the test when they collide with other values in the face of a difficult decision: choosing one value over another. In this scenario, while training the troops to value the goal and to endure the most difficult conditions, you also want to make sure that safety procedures (and the soldiers' lives) are preserved.

I felt quite alone under this great weight, and I needed some kind of lifeline. I needed something (or someone) to help me resolve this conflict, to help me see what I might be missing. A lifeline. Yes! That yard-and-a-half-long rope that connects two divers, the two buddies. We also call it a buddy line, the line that keeps the diving pair together in the deep and murky waters. That thin rope binds us together, literally and figuratively.

Suddenly it was clear to me. I raised my head, looked at the two team leaders and said: "The question each diver should ask himself is *not only* whether he can persevere when his own breathing becomes difficult and his consciousness foggy, but rather: should his *buddy* display signs of distress, would he be able to carry out the emergency rescue procedure? If the answer is yes, he is fit to save his buddy, then he should go on diving, endure, and hit home base. If the answer is no, he can't do it, then he should signal his buddy, ascend to the surface, and stop the dive at that moment."

In addition to the values of preserving life and the endurance required to fulfill the mission, a third value was identified and became part of the equation: the value of camaraderie and responsibility toward one another. The bond that is created in the baptism of fire was key in guiding our warriors to succeed and to stay alive. The protocols were changed for aborting a dive, and the considerations mentioned above became the standard in future training courses.

Along with my team's operational achievements, there is nothing in my service that gave me more satisfaction than this.

PART THREE
STILL WATERS RUN DEEP

The younger, uneducated version of me, a Navy SEAL holding a knife between his teeth, somehow knew that the best way to help myself would be to help others.

CHAPTER 11

Becoming the Shayetet Psychologist

The Best Way to Help Myself

Seven years later, in November 1999, I was back in the Shayetet, as the unit's psychologist.

Choosing this career path was a major life decision. It meant leaving SEAL operational command behind and taking on five to six years of study to become a clinical psychologist. It surprised me that I, an emotionally detached Navy SEAL with seemingly impenetrable walls of denial and repression, would even consider this career move. But it felt like the right decision, a decision I was ready to take on. I just knew. Perhaps it was my way to begin to breach the walls that had isolated me from my emotions for as long as I could remember. Perhaps it was my way to start my own process of healing myself.

The decision to make a major commitment didn't happen overnight. It was the outcome of a long process of self-discovery during my operational years. I was considered a successful SEAL and team leader. I was an accomplished combat diver with, at that time, a record number of sunken enemy ships under my belt. I was considered instrumental in training and motivating the warriors to achieve the highest operational ability, and I cherished the cohesive and close relationships with my soldiers and within my team. Spirits were almost always high, and the trust we had in each other enabled us to do almost anything.

When I became chief instructor and was put in charge of young SEAL commanders and trainees, I actually lost direct contact with the soldiers. I was handling the training curriculum and making sure the SEAL pipeline was productive, but I was spending more time at my desk than with the teams in training. I was more involved with unit headquarters and with the higher echelon of command. These were new, uncharted waters for me in which power struggles took up much of everybody's time and energy. While I felt a strong attachment to the Shayetet, I also felt like a fish out of water.

This feeling of being an outsider led me to question whether it was right for me to continue along the path of higher command. It was during this period that I started delving deeper into the rationale behind SEAL and special forces training. I became fascinated with the softer elements of warfare: What enables determination and stamina? How does a soldier overcome fear? *Should* a soldier overcome fear, or is it a necessary companion? I was intrigued by these and many more questions regarding behavior and decision making vis-à-vis enemy fire.

Captain Galinka was the commanding officer of the Shayetet. I requested an interview with him, and a few days later we sat in his office, separated by a large desk and years of experience. After some small talk, two cups of bitter coffee, and a discussion of several issues regarding the teams currently in training, he asked me, "Well, you asked for this meeting…what can I do for you?"

I remained silent for a short while, listening to my inner conflict: I didn't want to leave my role, but I needed to step out and challenge myself in a new direction. "I…I feel I'm not where I should be," I said. "I want to ask your permission to be relieved of my role as chief instructor. I want to terminate my contract and discharge from the military."

He thought for a while and said, "OK. So what are your plans for civilian life?"

"I want to become a psychologist," I replied.

Galinka was not an easygoing man, to say the least. Even though we did not interact on a daily basis, I got to know him fairly well and was familiar with his authoritative demeanor as the Shayetet commanding officer. In a few encounters at HQ, he expressed discomfort with my views of command. He was more of an old-school type. I felt we were not communicating on the same frequency. In addition, I had the feeling he didn't think highly of my achievements in my present role as chief instructor. I thought he would most likely accept my resignation, perhaps even welcome it. His next move caught me by surprise. He smiled and said, "Why discharge from the military? Go to school, get your degree, and come back here to resume the role of unit psychologist." It occurred to me that Galinka had anticipated what I had in mind. I said yes immediately and accepted his proposal.

The role of psychologist of the Shayetet had existed many years before I enlisted. The complex process of recruiting and training Navy SEALs and supporting commanders and teams necessitated a professional on board. Over the years, some of the most well seasoned and experienced clinical psychologists were assigned this role. Most had served as combat soldiers during their compulsory service, but none of them had served as a Navy SEAL prior to becoming the unit's psychologist.

In 1993, I was in my late twenties. I found the transition from a command role in the Shayetet to becoming a university student to be challenging, to say the least. I was back in school and back to normal civilian life. It took time to get used to life without the daily adrenaline rush to which I had become accustomed. I needed a few months to get the logistics in order. I had to take the psychometric exam, the Israeli version of the SAT (Scholastic Aptitude Test); I also had to improve some of my matriculation exam scores to reach eligibility status.

It was also during this period that Iris and I got married. After nine years together, it was time to formalize our relationship. Surrounded by a small circle of family and friends, we had a meaningful ceremony.

Neta, our eldest son, was born during my freshman year at university. For me, the child of the kibbutz, parenthood was a powerful game changer. Relaxing my contracted belly muscles, allowing myself to become affectionate, and accepting the anxiety of caring for a newborn were all good starters for a psychology major. It was a time of wonder, joy, and new love.

But letting go of my past had its price. My academic studies were going well and were rewarding, but at home, mainly at night, I experienced more and more intrusive thoughts, flashbacks, and nightmares. Waking up sweating in the middle of the night, my heart racing, I vividly relived events from my military service. It did not feel like just a memory. Not like the recall of some distant events or experiences. It felt as if it were happening again and again, in the present, with all the loss, the agony, the explosions, and the smells of blood and burning flesh. I felt a heightened sense of anxiety. The sense that something bad was about to happen. Some nights I dreamed that I was suffocating underwater – racing to the surface to bail out, hardly making it, almost drowning. I made a genuine effort, working hard to detach and to contain the emotional pain. I began to experience serious health-related issues. It was painful to watch the news on television, especially when reports of IDF casualties in Lebanon or elsewhere were aired. I was reexperiencing my own traumatic memories. I was wrestling with post-traumatic stress disorder (PTSD).

In hindsight, I now know that the choice to become a clinical psychologist and to work with traumatized soldiers was highly connected to my own journey to recovery and healing. The younger, uneducated version of me, a Navy SEAL holding a knife between his teeth, somehow knew that the best way to help myself would be to help others.

Coming Home

After more than six years in school, with intermittent periods of serving in the unit (mainly during summer vacations), being positioned as the Shayetet's psychologist felt like coming home. Warriors whom I had recruited and certified prior to my leave were now officers, team leaders, and company commanders. It was astounding to see just how fast time was passing and how the Shayetet was evolving and developing.

The Shayetet has its traditions, its norms, and its taboos. Like a modern-day order of knights, it encouraged a tendency toward the old ways of thinking. But with the advances of modern technology, things were rapidly changing. Sophisticated new equipment and fighting gear were incorporated into service. The young SEAL graduates were trained to function and make decisions in very extreme conditions. There was so much more they needed to learn now. Not only did they need to be made of the right stuff in terms of personality and character, but they also needed to be technologically savvy. Imagine a twenty-one-year-old made responsible for a highly sophisticated combat vessel, heavily armed and computerized with radar, sonar, and other sensors, as well as commanding a small crew to operate the vessel. In other navies, marine officers take on similar duties only after long years of training and operational service. In the Shayetet, recent graduates who had just completed the SEAL training course were given these responsibilities. Men who did not even have officer ranking.

They had to be smart, learn fast, and implement these new technologies under extreme conditions. They needed to sharpen their situational awareness. The maritime environment is constantly changing due to winds, currents, and moving vessels. Operational conditions on land are complex and dangerous. Moving between the different theaters of operation (sea, air, and land) makes operational conditions even more challenging. And of course, there is also the enemy to take into consideration.

As the unit's psychologist, I was now the professional in charge of the recruitment process. This included finding the right candidates and making sure the boot camp worked effectively. We were searching for people with the whole package to start the long vetting and training process. I was also overseeing the training process itself, in terms of what is sometimes referred to as stress inoculation: ensuring that the most effective coping mechanisms are developed and put into practice. It was also my job to provide assistance to soldiers and officers, should the need arise, in times of crisis or in personal matters.

In 1999, I began my tenure as unit psychologist, and I knew I had a lot to learn. I needed to review the decades-old practices that had worked until then: screening procedures, emergency interventions, leadership training, mental health screening, and support. I was familiar with some of the practices from my own experience as an operational soldier, commander, and instructor. But I needed to look at those practices from a new perspective. It was like reentering a familiar place but from a different angle. As a military leader, one tends to look at things through a sniper's telescope, focusing on the details and the logic necessary for the successful fulfillment of a military mission. As a psychologist, I had to complement that approach with a softer, process-oriented behavioral approach.

After some thought, I sensed that my challenge would be to merge both angles of vision. I knew that in order to succeed, I would need to be flexible and be able to move between the paradigms. I would need to adhere to the "no bullshit, down to business" Shayetet thinking but also be able to sense what was going on within the process of combat training. The next step would be to position myself to be able to influence and improve both the process and the outcome. Better recruitment and training would foster improved leadership, operational ability, and results.

My operational background was something no one could take away from me. I had a few war stories to tell. But I needed to take a step back from being one of "them" and, as the unit's psychologist, to relax the constricted muscles of my belly which represented the psychological defenses that had kept me alive. I needed to be able to identify the undercurrents of the Shayetet. I needed to sharpen my sensors so I wouldn't feel as if I were operating an assault boat without radar.

Part of the curriculum at the university included my own therapy sessions with a psychologist. This was just the excuse I needed to finally allow myself to open up. Slowly I began to understand and become aware of so many things I had kept hidden deep within myself. Loosening up my defenses, getting to know and embrace the pain that was hidden inside me all these years, and working through it with my therapist proved to be very meaningful and helped me feel more at home with myself.

When I started to practice psychotherapy as part of my clinical studies, it enhanced my healing and gave me a new sense of purpose. It felt as if everything was starting to fall into place. I felt that I was emotionally present and that my own self-awareness had sharpened. This enabled me to connect with my first clients and to help them with their own personal challenges.

Psychotherapy is the art of healing in which verbal exchange is the medium of self-exploration, support, and sharing emotions. In a secure setting, the client shares personal issues, conflicts, relationships, and dreams, opening new and old wounds. The therapist serves as a witness, as a sounding board and confidant to assist the client in his or her personal journey. During the therapeutic process, a bond is often formed between client and therapist. Within this safe relationship, the existing maladaptive emotional, cognitive, and behavioral patterns are identified and eventually transformed into new, adaptive ones.

One behavioral pattern that is often the focus of therapeutic work is how clients safeguard themselves in the face of anxiety, negative emotions, and traumatic life events. Mortality is a given. But most people repress the thought of their own inevitable death as well as the deaths of their loved ones. It is common to rationalize these thoughts in order to calm ourselves, using statistics or scientific facts to prove to ourselves that we (and our loved ones) are "OK." Some use the defense mechanism of projection – blaming others for faults of their own. Each person has a unique pattern of defense mechanisms that are applied in a similar manner, across different situations, over time.

Within my own maturation process, I recognized my defense mechanisms clearly: my detachment and emotional isolation were dominant in my psychological makeup. I also became aware that this same defense pattern was prevalent among my fellow Shayetet soldiers. When you are a fighter, endangering your life, these defense mechanisms are almost as important as your bulletproof Kevlar vest. You cannot function as a warrior if you are scared to death.

For this reason, I knew that while some of the soldiers would need my assistance, the therapeutic work would need to be focused and gentle and that these defense mechanisms needed to be respected in order for them to sustain operational efficacy. Stripping soldiers of their defenses might put them in danger. Mentally resilient people have highly efficient coping mechanisms but may find themselves on slippery ground when confronted with mission failure, the loss of a friend or friends in combat, or even personal issues such as a failed relationship. When a tragic or traumatic event hits close to home, those defenses may be penetrated and shaken. Then even the strongest special forces "superheroes" may be forced to confront their demons in the shape of their own fears and pain and are likely to experience anxiety and depression. These soldiers need support in strengthening their adaptive coping skills while, at the same time, preserving and respecting their battle-proven psychological defense mechanisms.

A Crossroads

After putting in long hours in the office on my first day as the unit psychologist, I decided to call it a day. It was early November, and the sun was just setting over the Mediterranean Sea. Before leaving for home, I decided to take advantage of the mild weather and the remaining daylight and to go for a workout. I started off running barefoot, as I always did, on the beach. With my swimming goggles strapped around my arm, I ran for a few miles, enjoying the breeze and soft sand beneath my feet. While I was running along the shoreline, the waves paving my route and wetting my feet, I became overwhelmed by a deep sense of accomplishment upon embarking on my new role. I had imagined and envisioned this day (after Captain Galinka's vision, of course) for many years.

It was almost dark when I walked into the cool Mediterranean water to complete the last leg of my workout. The sea was quiet and smooth and the water transparent. I started swimming and could see the symmetrical footprints of crabs on the seabed just below me. As I was swimming and breathing rhythmically, the last light was painting the clouds in the west in the most gorgeous colors – a breathtaking scene. But underneath, the water was already dark.

Then something unexpected happened. Over the years I had completed countless night swims and dives, some in dangerous, unwelcoming places.

During these dives I was focused on the mission, not allowing any other thoughts or emotions to sneak into my mind. This time was different. I thought, "What if I get a cramp in my foot? What if I can't swim? I'm totally alone here, and there's no one who can help me..." These thoughts were accompanied by an emotion that I had long forgotten. I was suddenly afraid.

It was like meeting an old friend – a companion who had been lost and was now knocking on my door. It was almost a joy for me to realize that this was happening. "Welcome, old buddy," I heard myself saying. I was alive and connected to my inner feelings, and it was OK. Now, I felt, I was ready to move on to my new role and to the next stage of my life.

Walking out of the sea, I stopped for a few seconds and just stood there, my feet feeling the soft, sandy seabed. The water was waist deep, the evening twilight having surrendered to a dark and beautiful night. I was facing the dimly illuminated Shayetet naval base, the barracks, the boat hangers, headquarters. The calm, dark sea around me. Countless times before, I had swum, dived, and sailed in these waters. I knew every sea current, beach, and sand dune in the Bay of Atlit and its surroundings. But this time felt different. At this meeting point between land and sea, I truly felt I was at a crossroads between my old life as a fighter and my new life as a certified clinical psychologist. Many emotions surfaced, including lost emotions, as I embarked upon my new and exciting role as the Shayetet psychologist, giving this experience a deep personal meaning.

The US Navy SEALs' insignia is the trident, the weapon of the mythological Greek god of the sea, Poseidon. It is also represented by the Greek letter *psy*, which bears a resemblance to the trident. Today, this letter also represents the science and trade of psychology.

At that moment, I felt the presence of a powerful spiritual force, perhaps my divine chaperone, blowing wind into the sails of my own journey. I looked back toward the dark sea, smiling to myself.

After a warm shower in the barracks, I returned to my office and in what seemed like a symbolic act, I opened the safe – which contained confidential reports and other classified material – and locked my personal handgun inside. I thought to myself: "I don't need this anymore." In less than a year, as matters turned out, I was proven wrong.

CHAPTER 12

Crisis Management

The Long Night

After a few weeks at my new job, I recognized that the Shayetet psychological protocols were operating like a well-oiled machine. This meant that no revolutionary modifications were called for that I could see. The two main challenges I did identify were:

1. Prepare a better crisis intervention and support plan.
2. Reduce the dropout rate during SEAL training.

Crisis intervention became a top priority on my list of challenges, most likely as a result of the devastating incident that had occurred ten years earlier when I was a team commander. This disastrous incident was the first time I had to cope with a catastrophe. As I sat at my desk in the Shayetet psychologist's office, I pictured the event as it had unfolded all those years ago. I could smell the blood, gunpowder, and the cold sea mist. I recalled the huge waves, the shouts, and the deafening blast. And I could feel the anguish, the sorrow, and the sense of loss that followed.

It was late February 1990, and the team was only a month away from graduation. That night's dive was dangerous, and to complicate matters, a storm was brewing. The waves rose higher and higher. The soldiers entered the water and started their dive. A few minutes into the dive, an attempt was made to abort the exercise. The waves were too high, and diving became dangerous, but it was too late. Two divers had drifted away from the rest of the team and were washed up onto a reef. The buddy line connecting the two divers had severed, and one of the divers was missing.

We launched a search and rescue operation as we were trained to do in such a situation. The level of distress heightened as time passed and we came to realize that the chances of finding the missing diver alive were slim to nonexistent. Hope, combined with a sense of urgency, prompted us to continue the search. It was dark, and we needed to illuminate the area. One of the soldiers on the beach tried to shoot a flare into the sky above us. He was holding an 84mm recoilless cannon, one that shoots both anti-tank shells and flares. This weapon is recoilless, meaning that while you aim and shoot the shell forward, an enormous thrust blasts backwards. It is imperative that no one be behind it when you fire.

Under extreme stress, people make mistakes. Sometimes, bad decisions made under duress cross the point of no return. Dotan was a young warrior, inexperienced with this type of weapon but eager to help. He fired the cannon in the right direction, but sadly, he placed the rear of the gun in his lap. I heard the explosion and then the shouts. Running in his direction, I saw Dotan lying on his back, his right leg missing, almost to his groin. Instinctively I knew that he would die from blood loss unless I acted fast. I had in my pocket an arterial tourniquet (or blocker) designed to stop arterial bleeding, but there was not enough of his thigh left to apply it. The directive in this case, which I had learned and drilled, was to close my fist and push hard against the side of the groin, where the main artery is, in order to stop the bleeding.

Dotan was in great pain and mumbling, "I can't believe I did this to myself." After long, agonizing minutes, the ambulance arrived, and Yaron and Ilan helped me put Dotan on the stretcher. They picked up the stretcher as I continued to apply pressure to Dotan's artery. While hoisting the stretcher into the back of the ambulance, I was pressed up against the side door, unable to get in alongside the wounded soldier. From this position, I could no longer apply pressure to Dotan's artery, so Yaron took over for me. Yaron, a trained combat medic, took hold of the open artery and squeezed it, stopping the bleeding. The back door of the ambulance slammed shut and they drove away, leaving me standing there, stunned. In a short while, the ambulance arrived at the hospital ER. Dotan survived.

While Dotan was on his way to the ER, I took on the responsibility of directing the F-4 Phantom jet fighter that had been called to assist in illuminating the area. Using the wireless radio, I directed the pilot where to drop flares in order to help us with the search and rescue operations. It was a long night. When morning came, we were still searching for the missing diver. I was covered with Dotan's blood, my uniform stiff and dirty, and I was bleeding emotionally from within.

Ziv Levy was the missing diver. His body was recovered later that morning. It had washed ashore in the Atlit Bay, a few hundred yards from where we had lost him. The pain was overwhelming.

As a young team leader, I now understood what it meant to be responsible for my soldiers' lives. But what really struck me was the absolute necessity to continue leading the team now, in this dire hour. I found my soldiers together in their barracks, their combat gear wet and scattered about. They looked lost. I talked with some of them, but I was confused myself.

It took me a while to realize that what they needed most was for me to be there and to take command. They needed me to be with them, share their grief, and move them to action. After much thought, I really internalized just how important military (or any) leadership is during times of crisis. Back in the barracks, nothing in the unit's rule book provided me with the tools for crisis intervention that would have been a great help to me in navigating these rough, uncharted waters.

Years later, in 1997, during one horrible night, we lost twelve warriors in an operation in Lebanon. I was still training as a clinical psychologist at the time, but I rushed to the Shayetet to help out. The sense of loss and the level of stress and trauma in the unit were understandably high. The officers and unit psychologist provided support to the young commanders and the surviving soldiers. We did the best we could. The urgency for formal crisis management tools was never more palpable.

My first challenge as unit psychologist in 1999 was to provide the tools of awareness and the procedures for crisis intervention. As I began my new role, I first needed to be accepted as a relevant figure so that the SEALs would respect my input. That part was relatively easy, since I was, myself, a member of the clan. I then set about trying to figure out how to approach the job and set the standards. It was the most urgent task on my to-do list, but I did not think I would need to implement these crisis intervention tools so soon.

The Invisible Bullet of Trauma
It was demoralizing and destabilizing to realize just how vulnerable were the lives of our warriors. Whether a soldier is shot in combat, lost in turbulent

enemy waters, or killed by accident during a training exercise, the results for the team are traumatic. One minute your fellow soldier is there, the next minute he is not, his life force ebbing from his ruined body. Those left behind inevitably feel deep pain, shock, and guilt over this terrible loss.

The survivor thinks about what happened and wonders if there was something he could or should have done to prevent the death. Feelings of guilt are often present. The next question that arises is: "How could this happen to *us?*" *Us*, the invincible Shayetet warriors we strive to be.

IDF special forces units are generally considered to be the very best that our society has produced. These young men are high achievers and strive to excel in whatever they do. A mention of this service on one's CV can be compared with a degree from Harvard or Yale. It ensures a good starting point for any career and will open doors. But unlike earning an Ivy League degree, serving as a member of a unit of the IDF special forces entails putting your life and the lives of your soldiers on the line, with the country's survival resting in your hands. As members of the special forces, we are trained to succeed; the other option is inconceivable. Operations are well planned and comprehensive, including the collection and use of high-end intelligence to ensure results. Every training and operational activity is debriefed thoroughly; thus Navy SEALs are constantly learning from experience and encouraging excellence.

We are trained to win. And we feel invincible.

It is no secret that war is risky business. As one of the most highly trained units with special fighting capabilities, the Shayetet is assigned to the most complicated and potentially dangerous missions. Since the unit's inception, dozens of Shayetet warriors have been lost in dark enemy waters, in the blazing fire of combat, and in diving accidents in the friendly but unforgiving waters near our naval base. When we go into combat, we put on our Kevlar bulletproof vests, helmets, and the protective illusion that nothing can happen to us – even though logic and rational thinking tell us otherwise. You cannot function and deliver results if you are scared to death. That is why, when an operation fails, when a warrior is injured or killed, it is so devastating to the team and unit.

The loss of a friend or even a near miss affects us deeply and leaves open wounds in our souls. Psychological trauma or post-traumatic stress is a real risk to soldiers in any military unit. Even the strongest and most resilient individuals can suffer post-traumatic stress. Core strength has little to do with it. When the invisible bullet of trauma hits, it may go unnoticed at first. One does not bleed or show any visible signs of injury, but nevertheless, life can become a prolonged nightmare for the victim of trauma and for his or her loved ones.

For me, the realization that I was dealing with my own traumatic experience came slowly. It took me years and hindsight to diagnose myself with PTSD. It was such a well-guarded secret, kept from others, kept from myself. I just worked harder, tried to distract myself from my bleeding internal self. The mood swings, disruptive sleep patterns, intrusive thoughts, and memories were part of the reality that I had to cope with. It was not a medical problem that could be treated.

One of the first things that a special forces soldier learns is that when things get tough, you need to get tougher. You simply cope. If you have to carry more weight, then you work harder and suffer through it. If your feet hurt, you just keep on going. Young people are usually not aware of that internal voice telling them that they are off course. Emotional situational awareness – the ability to understand that something bad is happening – is not fully developed. I wasn't aware that I was facing the repercussions of my military service and that I was distracting myself by doing what I always did – working hard and isolating my emotions.

When I became a therapist, I was able to start the process of healing. Not only could I for the first time tend to my own wounds, but my healing was further enhanced through helping others in their own healing journeys.

The IDF Combat Stress Unit

The IDF's Mental Health Center has a small therapeutic unit, designated for the diagnosis and treatment of soldiers who suffer combat-induced post-traumatic stress. Parallel to my service as the Shayetet psychologist, I provided therapy to soldiers who had returned physically from the battlefield, but who remained on the battlefield emotionally, twenty-four seven. While interviewing my new clients during the patient intake procedure, I was overwhelmed, time and again, listening to their stories. I was often struck by how familiar their stories were to my own experiences.

For many of us, time stopped, and every detail or task in our lives became terrifying and impossible to deal with and control. A shattered world, dangerous and uncertain. Guilt and shame, entangled within a broken soul.

Let's call him Joey. He completed his three years of mandatory service as an infantry combat soldier in the IDF and reentered civilian life. Ten years passed before he realized that something was very wrong. As he sat on the couch in my office during our first meeting, I told him a little about myself and prepared him for the intake procedure. I would note his personal details, history, and ask him about his complaint or symptoms.

I was wearing my uniform with the Shayetet bat wings on my chest. Joey looked at me, at my Shayetet insignia, and took a deep breath, leaned back, and said: "You're a warrior. You've been there…you will understand…" I nodded and remained silent. Joey wasn't anxious. He seemed detached, locked up, safeguarding his own intense emotions.

"Every night, sometimes a few times during the night and many times during the day, the images come back to me. It feels as if I'm experiencing the battlefield again and again. As if it's happening now. And I can't deal with it anymore…" Joey didn't move, but somehow, I felt him becoming more emotional. Something was opening up, I hoped.

"It was during a regular patrol near Jerusalem. I had done many of these before. Nothing special. It was near a major highway where Palestinians sometimes threw stones and Molotov cocktails at passing Israeli cars. A driver whose car was hit by a stone could easily lose control and crash. A Molotov cocktail could also burn passengers to death. Our mission was to stop them." Joey became anxious. I could see his face getting pale and his lips trembling.

"We spotted a few teenagers. They held bottles, maybe Molotov cocktails, and they started throwing them. They also threw stones at the cars. I shouted, '*Wakef!* [Arabic for "stop"]' and then fired one shot in the air. They didn't stop. I fired another shot. A young boy, perhaps eleven years old, fell. I hit him."

Joey did not know if the boy survived. The Israeli soldiers treated his wounds, and he was taken to the hospital. The next day, Joey was called to the brigade commander. "The colonel treated me nicely. He said that I had done the right thing and most probably had saved the lives of Israelis who had been driving on that road. He gave me a citation for distinction in action…"

Joey was getting very emotional. A tear ran down his cheek. It was the story of guilt, of getting the mission done and earning distinction, while inside he was bleeding. That boy had never left him, even after all these years.

During our weekly sessions, Joey and I took a journey, working through his intense emotions, following his invisible but deep psychological wound. Witnessing his pain, while connecting with my own, we began to uncover a new meaning to his traumatic experience.

During the process, I got to know him better, delving into his childhood and family background. I suggested possible links between long-ago events, prior to his military service, the actual shooting of the boy, and his post-military life. It was like weaving or mending a torn fabric, the results once again generating a coherent story.

About two years into therapy, Joey came into my office, sat down, and said: "I had a dream last night, but it was different... The boy was holding a gun. He shot back and..." Joey stopped and became thoughtful. "I can't remember what happened next," he said. Then he continued: "My father was a cop. He was like the town's sheriff. Everybody respected him. When I was a child, he got into trouble and was accused of using excessive force. He lost his job. It was a very hard time for the family and for me."

"How old were you when it happened?" I asked.

Joey had a puzzled look on his face and said, "I think I was eleven years old."

"And so was the boy that you shot," I said.

"Yeah...but how is that connected?" he asked.

"Well, your father, the sheriff, used excessive force, and you, then an eleven-year-old boy, got the flak. You and the family. The sheriff father you were so proud of suddenly becomes an embarrassment to the family. That could have been a major blow for you. Ten years later you are the sheriff, a soldier operating to enforce order. Using what you see as excessive force, you shoot an eleven-year-old boy..." I looked at Joey, trying to figure out if he was with me. He was.

"In a mysterious way, that poor boy who was shot was for you..."

"The boy symbolized myself," Joey said.

I nodded, waited a few long seconds, and said, "And you identified with that boy. It felt too close. Too personal."

This was one of our last sessions. I felt that the long process we had gone through enabled distance and insight. Joey could now let that boy rest and leave this terrible experience behind him. While this moment of closure unfolded for Joey, I felt a moment of personal revelation and could glimpse in my mind's eye another eleven-year-old boy coming close to being shot while hiding in a bush, one stormy Saturday afternoon in March 1978.

Following up with Joey, post-therapy, I understood that he was feeling and functioning much better. His PTSD symptoms were gone, most of the time. It was satisfying to see that within the secure sphere of our therapeutic alliance, Joey's trauma was worked through and left behind. I saw this as a shared journey even though I was the therapist and Joey the patient. Both of us were soldiers, wrestling with our past. Each in his own way and both of us together were able to create a narrative of moving forward, back to life. A narrative of "A time to kill, a time to heal."

CHAPTER 13

Creating a Culture of Wellness

A Caring Leadership

Therapists who assist traumatized patients can become traumatized themselves merely by the exposure to such pain and sorrow. To me, this exposure felt as if I were drinking cool water in the hot dessert. I was there, present, compassionate, and in a position to help. It was an ongoing process to learn how to provide individual therapy, to be alert and ready to assist any Shayetet warrior who might be hurt and in need of my help.

That was one part of the equation. I also needed to make sure that the Shayetet teams would be well taken care of, especially during times of loss.

The need to care for the men in these situations and to proactively intervene was not a given. The way most commanders saw it, the priority was to get the unit back to operational status as soon as possible, and this was usually achieved through intensive activity. The reasoning was that the teams should return to operational status immediately. They were sometimes sent out on an operational mission very soon after a traumatic event. Giving the men a chance to vent and share their emotions seemed risky and counterproductive, according to this school of thought. When I had faced similar situations as a young SEAL team leader, I had not known what else to do but follow my commanders' example and get the team back into action. As the unit's psychologist, I felt that it should be done differently.

Most commanders perceived a schism between the need to sustain mission preparedness and the need to care for the psychological well-being of the soldiers. Some held the belief that if you stop and allow the men to "lick their wounds," it might take them longer to return to operational readiness. If you get the team right back into action, they will just "get over" the traumatic event and resume their operational duties. Those who agree with this view believe that, on the military scale, the mission is more important than the individual soldier, hence the justification in risking the soldiers' well-being in the name of operational preparedness. Others believe that it would be beneficial for the soldiers' psychological well-being to pause after a traumatic event and share and vent their feelings. In other words, this school of thought promotes the notion that the military mission can wait, at least temporarily.

While both of these viewpoints had been common in the Shayetet for many years, I sensed that both schools of thought lacked something. I believed that caring and intervening in real time, in a predetermined and proactive way, would both improve the psychological well-being of the soldiers and allow the unit to resume operational status quickly and more effectively.

For every military entity, winning the war is the highest priority. For the IDF, there is no other option. That was never in question. Having said that, every soldier knows he might have to pay dearly for victory and even more dearly in defeat. It is my belief that it is essential to preserve the psychological wellness of the soldiers returning from the battlefield. It is an integral component of our ability to win.

When I took my post as Shayetet psychologist at the end of 1999, the Israeli-Palestinian political process was progressing, and many thought we were heading toward a peaceful era. That thought was short-lived. A few months later, the IDF withdrew from Southern Lebanon, the 2000 Camp David peace talks between Israeli prime minister Ehud Barak and Palestinian Authority chairman Yasser Arafat hosted by President Bill Clinton failed, and the smell of trouble was in the air. As the second Palestinian uprising gained momentum in October 2000, my unit was brought in to participate in ground-based special operations in the territories under Palestinian Authority control. Palestinian suicide bombers exploded in Israeli cities almost daily, and our task was to stop them. The Shayetet's flexibility and rapid response capability were called upon to thwart the deadly attacks. There were many arrests and hits on Palestinian terrorists. We also had our share of failures. The enemy was smart and determined. We lost a number of our finest men in combat during this uprising.

At unit headquarters, we prepared the schedules for the teams after their return from a mission. A few hours of sleep, a good meal, and a physical workout would be beneficial in helping them create some distance from the operation. After operations in which there were close calls or in which soldiers were wounded or killed, or after a failed mission, we would analyze the operation and focus on the soldiers and commanders involved. We assessed how the outcome of the mission was perceived by the participants, in terms of feelings of responsibility, guilt, or the placing of blame for a mistake or a wrong decision.

We analyzed the minute details of the battle: who did what, who didn't operate according to plan, and who was the closest to the fallen when the incident occurred. It was also determined who was on close terms with the injured or killed soldier. We thought it was critical to discern who felt guilty and who felt the heaviest sense of loss within the team. The process of mapping out the circles of impact and what happens to the soldiers internally is at the heart of managing a crisis and the crux of military leadership. The psychologist's role was to assist commanders in determining who had been hit by the invisible bullet of trauma. In such cases, an intervention led by the team leaders, in the guise of a military-style debriefing, was conducted.

During this challenging and tumultuous period, in which we suffered many losses, I had the privilege of working with an extraordinary commanding officer, Ram Rothberg. He was the commander of the Shayetet at the time. Back in the 1980s, Ram (then a young team leader) was my commander during the last phase of my SEAL training. He was the kind of commander with whom you could communicate at eye level, meaning eye to eye as opposed to hierarchically. Ram understood the need to care for the warriors after a mission. With his support, we introduced the model of critical incident stress management (CISM), an intervention framework that was developed in the United States in the 1970s. We conducted such interventions for soldiers, for the teams, and for the unit as a whole.

In a briefing room, the men sat in a circle, their eyes red from lack of sleep or from tears shed in grief over the loss of a close buddy. They sat quietly for a while, each immersed in his own thoughts and feelings. This is not a psychological intervention conducted by a psychologist, but a military debriefing led by the operational commander. I was present to assist and to coach the commander.

Here's how such a meeting might look.

Team commander: "It's Wednesday night. A little more than twenty-four hours have passed since the battle. Our mission was accomplished, but we paid a heavy price. We all know what happened. It's a hard time for all of us, so don't stay alone with the pain. For the next few hours, we're going to sit and talk."

Me: "This session is part of our combat procedure. We train, get the gear ready, and brief before a mission. After the mission, we debrief the operational, technical, and logistical sides in order to draw conclusions and learn to do better next time. Now we're going to debrief the emotional side of this painful event."

A brief pause, then I would add: "Ground rules: Confidentiality. Everything said here stays here. You only talk if you want to. You are invited to share. We do not criticize or debate. Feelings are personal."

During the debriefing sessions, these macho guys, not known to be talkative types, would sit with their team for two or three hours, venting and sharing their thoughts and feelings. The issue of survivors' guilt would surface again and again. Some felt they could have done more. Some, who were not even on the mission, felt guilty for not having been there.

Our Navy SEALs are nicknamed "men of silence." This was a new experience for them, and during this debriefing intervention, they learned how to share their feelings, how to relate to their teammates, and, in a sense, how to talk. Those who had been the most resistant during these sessions were later the first to acknowledge their significance.

Once you've shared your thoughts and feelings, you come to realize that you're not the only "crazy," sad, or anxious person in the room, on your team, or in the unit. The strong bond between these men, forged in the line of fire and in the depths of the ocean, provided a safe environment for them to open up. The goal was to share and to get the team back to operational preparedness ASAP. Most important in this type of intervention was the empowerment of young military commanders. They became better leaders. Understanding that the mission is not only about professional skills but also about caring for the men and the teams has enriched their command toolbox and set new levels of operational competence.

In the early 1990s, while I was chief instructor and deputy commander of the SEAL training school, I put in many hours with young SEAL team leaders, focusing on their operational leadership while overseeing the training of their teams. Ten years later, as the Shayetet psychologist, I felt that cultivating their crisis management tools and helping them work through events of crisis and loss would empower and inspire them to become better team leaders.

With these soft command skills, in addition to the leadership tools in their boxes, they would prove to be better, more professional, and more focused mission commanders.

Commanders who genuinely care for those who follow them into battle plant the seeds of something very precious in their men. What creates the inner strength necessary to motivate a warrior? What is necessary to boost a soldier's inner strength so that he will take the initiative, think independently, and explore other possibilities on the stage set before him? The example of caring leadership endorses the feelings of trustworthiness and being appreciated as individuals. It encourages the contribution of the warrior to the team. This kind of leadership can propel one forward and strengthen resilience, as well as inspiring operational excellence.

Reducing the Dropout Rate for Trainees

Personnel recruitment for elite units is a process that begins with screening volunteers who, after being selected, go on to participate in the boot camps. Only those who survive boot camp continue on to basic infantry training after their formal induction. Then they have to pass the Basic Underwater Demolition/SEALs (BUD/S) training, which, as described earlier, many trainees find too hard to endure. The dropout rate is high. Even surviving the Shayetet BUD/S training is not a guarantee that you will complete the course. Trainees can be ousted at any time during training. Some have even been let go as late as the last week of the twenty-month course.

It seemed to me that the rate of success in the Shayetet training course was extremely low. Only 20 to 30 percent completed the rigorous course. I thought that this did not make good economic sense. I felt that the generous resources allocated to recruitment should be reviewed and used more efficiently. Training costs money, for ammunition, gasoline for the boats, oxygen, combat gear, manpower, and other costs. Not to mention the time and effort invested by the instructors and recruits themselves. It did not seem reasonable that most of these young soldiers, considered to be Israel's finest, did not make it to the end of this grueling course.

After analyzing the recruitment and training pipeline, I came to realize that the high rate of failure was rooted in the inner culture of the unit. Every organization has a culture, a set of traditions, core values, and a language of its own. This culture has been shaped over the years by the successes and failures of its operations. It is a huge challenge to change and modify organizational culture. But I thought that this culture needed modifications in order to get better results.

The IDF General Staff Reconnaissance Unit or Sayeret Matkal, our sister and "rival" elite unit, was inspired by the Palmach – the pre-state underground military organization that later became the foundation of the IDF. The Palmach was known for its informal structure and for its lack of strict military discipline. This culture, adapted by the Sayeret, encouraged innovation, creativity, and accountability. In their training (as long and hard as ours), it is their inner motivation, inspired by their commanders, that inspires the teams to distinction. Rarely did they apply punishment or use harsh discipline.

The Shayetet was founded by veterans of the British Army. Some of the Shayetet founders enlisted and served in the Jewish Brigade during World War II. They fought against the Nazis in Europe and North Africa and brought to the Shayetet a culture of harsh discipline. When I was a trainee, we were under constant scrutiny and punished for minor transgressions, most of which were common in training. It was a culture that demanded discipline, precision, determination, and stamina, with mission fulfillment being the ultimate goal.

I was confident that there was a way to maintain the highest operational and professional levels and lower the 70 to 80 percent dropout rate at the same time. I also suspected that the carrot and stick approach needed refinement, that transgressions should be acknowledged but not necessarily punished so harshly. I believed that bolstering the soldiers' inner motivation and encouraging responsibility would help them attain higher achievement and accountability.

But I needed a way to prove this idea and convince my commanders that this could work. I needed a metaphor to help them visualize the possibility. Looking out my office window, I watched the soldiers training, operating Zodiac rubber boats in the sea. Then it clicked. In the late 1970s, the Shayetet stopped using the old Zodiac rubber boats as operational vessels. They were powered by two outboard motors, which were noisy, prone to technical failure, and less efficient than more advanced vessels. The experience of Operation Moses prompted the upgrade from outboard to inboard, jet-propelled motor vessels.

In 1979, the Israeli Navy, the Shayetet, and the Mossad worked together to carry out a daring operation. Operation Moses brought the first Ethiopian Jews to Israel, smuggling them out of Africa. Because of the political turmoil in Northeast Africa, the Jewish community in Ethiopia was in great peril, and Israeli prime minister Menachem Begin gave the order to save this community. That was the beginning of a modern-day exodus.

Some of my Shayetet buddies were recruited and joined agents of the Mossad in the operation. They built and operated a small resort on a beautiful beach on the Red Sea coast of Sudan, not far from the Ethiopian border. During the day, European tourists enjoyed the sun, sea, and other activities offered by the resort. At night, the resort's employees, actually Mossad agents and Shayetet warriors, smuggled the Ethiopian Jews into trucks and headed toward predetermined beaches in Sudan. The Ethiopian Jews were then delivered to the awaiting Israeli naval vessels, which sailed northward to safety in Israel. Navigating in the shallow waters, near coral reefs, necessitated the use of reliable boats, better than the Zodiacs. This is when the navy introduced the rigid inflatable boats (RIBs). These were small, hard-bottomed boats with inboard jet-propelled engines. These boats eventually replaced the old Zodiacs as operational SEAL delivery boats.

While the story of Operation Moses is powerful and has become part of the ethos of Israel's nation building, the reason I chose to tell it in this context had to do with the evolution of operational methods. Zodiac rubber boats with outboard engines had been in use for decades. They probably would still be in service if an urgent tactical need (Operation Moses) hadn't arisen. The introduction of the new RIB boat with an inboard jet engine proved to be more efficient and stealthy and therefore became the standard operational vessel.

The analogy of outboard versus inboard engines is the one I used to try to convince the Shayetet command and instructors that we needed to change our training paradigm. We needed our trainees to be empowered by internal motivation rather than threats and punishment. I explained that harsh discipline and the stick were analogous to the outboard motor. It makes a lot of noise, is not energy efficient, and often fails (as evident in the 80 percent dropout rate of trainees).

Empowerment through positive reinforcement, mentoring, and encouraging responsibility (thereby enhancing inner determination) is the inboard motor. It gets the job done with much less background noise.

Incorporating this new paradigm into the existing training program was not a simple transition to make. The harsh attitude and strict discipline (the old paradigm) toward trainees sustained the idea of the instructor as gate-keeper. My idea was to turn the instructor into a mentor, the objective being the encouragement of personal growth, empowerment, and boosting the professional fighting capability of the soldiers, thereby lowering the dropout rate. There is an inherent conflict between these two paradigms. Either you ask yourself, "Is he fit to be among our warriors?" or, "How can I help him become a better warrior?"

In order to apply a paradigm shift from sorting to nurturing, we needed to change the perception of the training staff regarding their role. They needed the practical tools to mentor the trainees. By reframing their mission as facilitating success and inner motivation while maintaining the role of gatekeeper, we slowly started the shift. But the hard and risky part was still ahead: as long as we recruited a large number of trainees and expected only a small number of graduates, the dropout rate would not decrease. On the other hand, if we started out with fewer soldiers and were unable to lower the dropout percentage, our combat teams would not have enough soldiers to carry out their missions.

That was the risky part, and I had to persuade my commanding officers that this could actually work. It was decided to gradually reduce the number of trainees accepted to the SEAL training course. It worked. Reducing the number of trainees in each consecutive class created a growing success rate. As dropout rates decreased, we had more time to nurture and facilitate the personal and professional growth of the soldiers. The outcome was evident in the improved fighting capacity of the graduating teams.

This was a long process that played out over a three-year period in which there were small successes and huge challenges. It was not an easy transition for a young SEAL graduate who had become an instructor to fight the urge to practice the same punishments he had endured as a trainee. The challenge was to form new empowerment traditions.

During my first year as the Shayetet psychologist, I worked very hard mentoring the trainers to adopt this new way of thinking. The first teams to enter this new training paradigm graduated in late October 2000. It was at this time that the second Palestinian uprising began with a surge of suicide bomb attacks across Israel. The young teams were thrown into combat earlier than we expected. Within a few weeks, they spearheaded a Shayetet offensive against the suicide bombers and against those who sent them. The younger teams joined the more experienced teams, and they successfully passed this baptism by fire. They were better than good; they were excellent.

CHAPTER 14

Operational Again

The Hostage and Crisis Negotiation Unit

With my gun hidden deep inside the safe in my office and my attention directed toward implementing the changes in the SEAL recruitment and training pipeline, I thought that I had left my operational tenure behind me.

My former teammates and colleagues were now either holding leading command positions in the Shayetet or in other units or had demobilized and were immersed in their civilian lives. I had my new day job as the Shayetet psychologist. Of course I remained connected with the unit's operational work and often joined training sessions with the teams, but mostly, I was trying (not too successfully, I must admit) to find the balance between the long days and nights at the base with being a father and a husband at home. Neta, our eldest son, was nearly seven when Ori, our second son, joined the family in the fall of 2000. I remember a moment, one moment, when I had the feeling that everything was falling into place. I was personally and professionally where I wanted to be. I thought that perhaps now I could lean back, smile, and feel a sense of accomplishment. As it turned out, this feeling was short-lived.

As the political and military situation continued to deteriorate with renewed hostilities, I felt the need to contribute my share. I looked for a way to bring my newly acquired professional skills into play together with my operational experience and to make an impact. I wanted to be operational again.

As a young boy, and later as a teenager, I loved working with ropes and cords. At sea, when setting sail, ropes are used and handled all the time. It fascinated me to tie various knots, but most of all to untie and open the tangles. Facing such a muddle, it's hard at first to know where to start. It looks like a big mess, with no apparent starting point. I would sit down, look at the ropes, get my fingers into the tangle, and start working.

Helping people in complex situations is like untying a tangled rope, requiring patience, endurance, analytic skills, and intuition. You must be willing to experiment and try different methods to see what works. You also need to be flexible enough to change direction when you get stuck. In most cases, the use of force to resolve situations like these will get you nowhere. If you cut the rope, it will become useless. If you pull hard, stronger knots will form that will become impossible to disentangle.

Armies use force. This is what war and military action is all about. But in modern warfare, especially in urban or suburban areas, it has been shown time and again that the use of excessive force can get you further entangled and can lead to disastrous outcomes.

Carl von Clausewitz, the Prussian general and military theorist who stressed the psychological and political aspects of war, defined war as "the continuation of diplomacy by other means…" Those "other means" refer to the use of military force. Historically, wars are fought in order to achieve political goals when diplomacy stalls or fails. When the use of military force has run its course and the goals have either been achieved or not, diplomacy is again applied to negotiate a ceasefire between the hostile sides and to reach a new agreed reality.

In modern conflicts, the distinction between the use of hard (military) power and soft (diplomacy, negotiation) power is less clear cut. In today's world, there are limitations to the use of force. The Western world has become very sensitive to the issue of civilian populations being kept out of military conflict. Non-state actors, such as terrorist organizations, commonly act from within civilian populations and target civilians, thus proving a challenge for military forces. Any encounter with them will likely result in the injury and death of innocents. This fact is exploited by the terrorists, who are well versed in the value of optics. Their objective is to manipulate the media to air such incidents, thereby bringing their plight to the awareness of a wide audience. The media plays into this and projects a biased picture of events that does not add to the understanding or the resolution of the conflict.

The limitations of military force in populated areas has made it necessary to develop alternative ways of thinking and applying soft power as an integral part of the military campaign. A military entity is required in order to confront barricaded terrorist gunmen or hostage situations as well as to deliver messages to the enemy.

The IDF Hostage and Crisis Negotiation Unit was first established in the 1970s. The urgent need for such a unit became paramount after the devastating terrorist attack in the northern Israeli town of Ma'alot in 1974. Dozens of high school students were held hostage by Palestinian terrorists in a school building. The terrorists demanded the immediate release of Palestinian prisoners held in Israeli prisons. While negotiations were underway, the military was preparing the tactical option. In an attempt to free the hostages, Sayeret Matkal teams stormed the building, and a terrible shootout ensued in which twenty-two youngsters were murdered by the terrorists.

This massacre has remained an open wound for decades. Not only for the bereaved families, but also for those who were in charge of the attempted rescue operation. Lieutenant Colonel Giora Zorea, Zaro's son and my mother's classmate from Maagan Michael, was the commander of the Sayeret during the Ma'alot massacre. After the loss of his two younger brothers, the tragic outcome of this event was a burden he would carry for many years. After this incident, Giora committed himself to strengthening the IDF's counterterrorism abilities and served for many years, reaching the rank of general. During those years, changes and advances in the Israeli counterterrorism forces led to the formation of new units, one of them the hostage negotiation unit that would complement and facilitate additional courses of action.

Colonel Lior Lotan served as an officer in Sayeret Matkal, the General Staff Reconnaissance Unit. In October 1994, Nachshon Wachsman, a Golani Infantry Brigade soldier, was abducted and held hostage by Palestinian terrorists in a small village near the Palestinian City of Ramallah, north of Jerusalem. In an attempt to free Wachsman, the Sayeret stormed the house where he was held. The force lost the element of surprise, delayed by the breaching of the front door. Wachsman was immediately shot and killed. A fierce fight ensued. Lior and his team managed to kill the terrorists, but a young and highly heralded officer, Nir Poraz, was lost, and Lior was badly injured in the effort. Five years later, Lior was assigned to reorganize the Hostage and Crisis Negotiation Unit. Around that time, I contacted him, and in what seemed to be the shortest telephone interview ever, I introduced myself and asked to join the team. He immediately invited me to come on board.

The IDF Hostage and Crisis Negotiation Unit consisted of academics in the fields of radical Islam and terrorism, lawyers and mediators, psychologists, fluent speakers of Arabic trained in negotiation tactics, and intelligence analysts. All were experts in their fields. Most had backgrounds in special operations forces. While we all had careers and held day jobs, we also maintained reserve emergency positions. When an emergency was brewing, the team would be called up immediately. During a crisis, the unit takes on a life of its own. It's sort of a mixture of a think tank and a SWAT team. We brainstormed and debated to come up with the best possible ideas which could then be translated into operational solutions.

The core mission of the hostage negotiation unit is to negotiate with terrorists – to resolve these high-profile, highly sensitive, and dangerous crisis situations. Preferably peacefully.

The classic scenario is one in which hostages are held in a building, a bus, a ship, or an airplane. Hostage taking can be seen as *instrumental* to the Palestinian cause, an attempt to extort the release of terrorists serving long sentences in Israeli prisons. It can also be *declarative* – to create and sustain a dramatic event in order to exploit media coverage, thus raising awareness of the struggle against Israel.

The bottom line is that these situations are risky to all involved – hostages, SWAT teams, and perpetrators alike. There is also a strategic challenge involved here. Should we give in to the terrorists' demands, Israel's deterrence is weakened, as is its sense of resilience.

Our job is to arrive at the scene as soon as possible, make contact with the terrorists, try to stabilize the fragile situation, and attempt to facilitate a peaceful resolution. When a peaceful resolution seems impossible, we try to manage the crisis and help mitigate the risk as much as possible.

Lior, the unit's commander, and Doron, his deputy and successor, ran the show. After about a year of recruiting, training, and running simulations, we learned to work well as a team. Besides the unit's core role, Lior and Doron managed to position the unit as a leading "soft power" think tank and crisis resolution team, working with the IDF's highest echelon of command. As the Palestinian uprising gained momentum, we were also called upon to take part and contribute to the effort.

Tactical Negotiation

An example of such a situation took place one year after Operation Defensive Shield, in the summer of 2003. An Israeli taxi driver, Eliyahu Gur-El, was abducted and held hostage in an unknown place in the Palestinian-held territories of Judea and Samaria. As his disappearance and the uncertainty regarding his situation turned into a suspected abduction, the Hostage and Crisis Negotiation Unit was activated. In the days that followed, together with Sayeret Matkal, the General Staff Reconnaissance Unit, we prepared a negotiation and deployment strategy at a military base near Jerusalem. As intel started to aggregate, it was believed that Gur-El was alive. We waited for more information to come our way.

On day two of Gur-El's disappearance, a phone call was received at his family's house. One of our negotiators answered the call. A man speaking Arabic, who called himself George, said that he was holding Eliyahu and that his demands for Gur-El's release would follow shortly. A second call soon followed. George demanded the release of two thousand Palestinian prisoners, all of whom were serving sentences in Israeli prisons. He threatened to kill Gur-El if his demands were not met. In the background, we could hear the cocking of a gun, or something that sounded like it.

In the meantime, the Israeli Security Agency, the Shin Bet, was working to collect intel and locate the abductors, looking for the thread that would guide them and enable the Sayeret teams to prepare a tactical option. We were in charge of profiling the event and building a profile for George. The questions that we asked ourselves were: Is George's demand for the release of prisoners really instrumental (i.e., was this an instrumental hostage taking, undertaken with the goal of achieving a concrete goal)? Is he really acting to free his brothers held in Israeli prisons, or does he have a different agenda? How stable is the situation, and to what extent can we expect it to remain stable? Do we have time? Can we buy time? And if so, how? Time is of the essence in a hostage situation because gathering intel, preparing a tactical option, and executing a rescue operation all take time.

We needed to sustain the conversation and to start forming some kind of a "give and take" relationship with George. This, we hoped, would help us create a tactical psychological profile of him (and other possible abductors). And, oh, yes – our main mission was to buy time.

George hung up. Two short phone conversations, a total of under twenty-five minutes. This was what we had to work with. We needed to understand who this "bad guy" was. I am not a fluent Arabic speaker, so I initially listened very carefully to the "music" and emotional tone of the conversation. Then I read the translation of the conversations. It was obvious that George was not displaying the demeanor of a well-trained and organized terrorist. He seemed emotionally unstable, and the way in which he tried to handle this high-profile, dangerous situation exposed nuances that captured my ear and attention.

Hostage Negotiations 101 – the basic playbook used by the FBI Crisis Negotiation Unit and by their British counterparts in New Scotland Yard – defines the first steps of hostage negotiation as follows:

1. Make contact, build rapport (if possible).
2. Present the hostage taker with a reality check. No, you cannot get everything you are asking for (safe conduct, release of prisoners, $10 million, and immunity).
3. Next, try to tone down the importance of the situation, portray it as a local infraction, as a "misdeed gone wrong" rather than as a strategically high-profile event.

This would seem to make sense when the adversary is someone we consider "normal." George (a name we were sure was an alias) was not. My impression was that George was displaying erratic behavior. As far as I could tell, George was probably not psychotic, but I got the sense that he seemed to have lost touch with the realities of the situation, that he wasn't thinking logically. Analyzing the way in which he communicated with our negotiator led me to suspect that his ability to connect with others was impaired. When our negotiator tried to set the boundaries of the situation, to achieve common ground for the discourse and establish with George some kind of basic give and take, he remained rigid and showed very little mental flexibility. This pattern of behavior resonated as being similar to a certain subtype of personality that is not well organized. We would have to be extra careful in playing ball with George and be prepared to bend the rules of negotiations as deemed fit in these circumstances.

With this tentative profile, my recommendations to the negotiators were to alter the standard tactics in communicating with the hostage taker and act in a very different manner from the way we were trained. Given the glitches in George's perception, there was the potential threat that he would become enraged and resort to violence. I thought it would be better to refrain from setting boundaries; I suggested containment as the leading negotiation strategy. Instead of "toning down" the event and minimizing its importance, I suggested "joining" George in his fantasy, playing along with him, and then guiding him toward making a deal. I thought it would be the safest way to buy time. I hoped that he would eventually agree to strike a deal and create a tactical operational opportunity.

I spoke to the negotiators over the phone, and I could almost visualize their raised eyebrows in reaction to what I suggested. It was counter to the textbook method of managing this kind of situation and to how they had been trained. Nevertheless, this negotiation path was chosen. It was not easy to explain our understanding of George's personality and of the situation to the commanding officer, but I managed to convince the general.

After four days of negotiations, we managed to close a deal and persuade George to arrange a meeting point. He felt confident enough to show up and was immediately seized and handcuffed by undercover police agents. George then led the Sayeret to the place where Gur-El was being held. The Sayeret stormed the compound. Eliyahu was found in a deep underground chamber used to store rainwater. He was liberated and taken to safety. He was in a state of shock, but otherwise healthy. He could now return to his family. I watched as Eliyahu was being examined by a doctor in the ambulance, and I thought about the long road he would now face in his journey to psychologically recover from this traumatic experience.

Suicide Bombers

The Palestinian suicide bombers, held in high regard by their own society, spearheaded the Palestinian struggle against Israel. During the second Palestinian uprising, between October 2000 and mid-2002, over a hundred suicide bombers exploded in Israeli cities, spreading death and terror. Many more would-be suicide bombers were captured or killed before they were able to carry out their attacks. The Palestinian "brothers" or handlers of these young people acted to recruit, train, and indoctrinate them into becoming *shahidim* (martyrs). When these young men "graduated," they were sent off to blow themselves up and murder Israelis.

Some of the recruiters who trained and sent the suicide bombers to attack and kill innocent Israelis were hunted for years by Israel's security agencies and special forces. A few were responsible for the murder of hundreds.

Using advanced intelligence, our forces were able to locate the arch-terrorists in their hiding places in the Palestinian-controlled territories. A stealth force from one of the elite units would be sent to infiltrate the town or village and lay siege to the hideout, usually at night. The soldiers would call for the terrorists to surrender. More often than not, they would refuse, and a shootout ensued. For years, the IDF ethos of engagement dictated storming the house. This was a dangerous undertaking, and a heavy price was paid in the number of soldiers and commanders who were wounded or killed during these exchanges.

Later the terms of engagement changed: the first thing was to call out to the terrorists to surrender and to evacuate the uninvolved citizens from the area. Only after the terrorists refuse to surrender is heavy fire used, and if necessary, the house is leveled. During some of these barricading events, the Hostage and Crisis Negotiation Unit was called in to negotiate with the terrorists, to try to convince them to lay down their arms and surrender.

Operation Defensive Shield

As the second Palestinian uprising gained momentum, more and more suicide attacks occurred. March 2002 was the peak, with thirty Palestinian suicide attacks in Israeli cities. The Israeli economy was nearly brought to a standstill, and normal life took on a surreal appearance. People stayed close to home and avoided riding buses (many attacks occurred on crowded buses) or eating in restaurants. It felt as if Israel was losing control of the situation. On March 27, during the Passover Seder in the banquet hall of a hotel in the coastal city of Netanya, two suicide bombers exploded, leaving 35 people dead and 140 more injured. The next day, Israel went to war: in Operation Defensive Shield, Israel launched an offensive attack aimed at eradicating terrorism in the Palestinian territories of Judea and Samaria (the "West Bank").

IDF forces stormed the Palestinian territories and its major cities. The plan was to surround and enter each city simultaneously, compelling the armed Palestinian men to barricade themselves in one place, from which we would try to convince them to surrender. The last part, trying to talk them into surrendering, was our job.

By that time, the gun I had locked away in my office safe was just a memory. I was now fully equipped with a Kevlar bulletproof vest, an M4 assault rifle, a Glock pistol, a helmet, and everything necessary to put the finishing touches to my counterterrorism combat gear.

We operated in many locations during the long weeks of this operation. Many of the team were in Bethlehem negotiating with Palestinians who held worshipers hostage in the Church of the Nativity, one of Christianity's most sacred sites. Then came the battle of Jenin.

Jenin is a Palestinian city in northern Samaria. It was known to harbor many workshops in which agricultural fertilizers were converted into C-4 explosives and others in which suicide vests were manufactured. The city provided shelter to hundreds of armed terrorists, completing this deadly chain of terror. On the third day of battle, IDF forces closed in on the refugee camp, in the downtown alleyways of Jenin. The fight was costly to our forces. We suffered many casualties. There were many casualties on the other side as well. It was intense, close-contact combat, with the IDF forces progressing from house to house, engaging Palestinian gunmen while doing their utmost to avoid wounding innocent civilians in the vicinity.

I was in the Shayetet base in Atlit when Doron, the deputy commander of the Hostage and Crisis Negotiation Unit, called and asked me to join him. "We are going to work in Jenin," he said on the phone. I drove to Megiddo, the biblical site of Armageddon, leaving my car at a military base near the checkpoint, just miles from Jenin. The third team member to join us on this mission was Oded, one of the most experienced officers on the team. Oded and I had known each other since childhood. We grew up on the same kibbutz and were about the same age.

We were driven into the Jenin fighting zone in an armored vehicle. The refugee camp was dense, with narrow alleyways winding between four- and five-story houses. Some of the houses had already been torn down, and there were tons of debris strewn about. The air was heavy with smoke. It felt and smelled like war.

Our mission was to minimize casualties of soldiers and uninvolved citizens. To achieve this goal, we had to convince the barricaded Palestinian gunmen to surrender and lay down their arms.

It was no easy task. The high-ranking officers at the front command post outside Jenin were skeptical: "The Palestinians will fight to the last bullet... Jenin will be their last stronghold, their Masada," they said. They were referring to Masada, the fortified stronghold built by King Herod the Great more than two thousand years ago near the Dead Sea. During the Roman conquest of the Holy Land, Jewish warriors were besieged on the mountain for three years. They eventually killed themselves so as to not be killed or sold into slavery by the Romans.

Our experience in this type of standoff led us to believe that this idea could work. Few people really desire to die, and even the most radical and determined terrorists, given the right legitimization and context, would choose life. They didn't trust us, but that didn't mean we couldn't influence them to surrender and live. We knew that in order to induce them to surrender, the scenario would have to be respectful. It had to be understood that there was no other choice but to surrender and that the Palestinian leadership would undoubtedly regard it as such. Surrender would be the honorable choice. This surrender needed to be backed up by a clear and deferential procedure.

The fighting in Jenin continued as we made plans to begin our negotiation. Gunshots from both sides could be heard in the distance. AH-1 Cobra assault helicopters were visible, providing support to the ground forces while firing missiles and shooting shells at specific targets.

The battlefield has a distinct smell. A combination of gunpowder, rotting garbage and dust, and oh, yes, the smell of human feces and fear. Accompanied by Golani infantry soldiers, we took shelter in an empty Palestinian house. We were briefed by the battalion commander and one of his company commanders, Major Avihu Yaakov. Avihu was a much-admired Shayetet team leader who was assigned to Golani to assume his next operational role. We shook hands as our eyes met in the darkened room. Avihu looked tired but determined. After the short briefing, we nodded goodbye to each other. Three weeks later, during a battle with armed terrorists in the Palestinian city of Nablus, the battalion commander was badly wounded. Avihu was killed.

We proceeded with our mission. Using a loudspeaker, we called out to the Palestinians. It was just before dusk, during the twilight hour. The twilight hour has the potential of being the most depressing time of day, in which one's stress coping mechanisms are at a low point. You are tired and begin thinking about loved ones and the desire to go home.

We started by calling out in Hebrew: "All IDF forces cease fire!" We wanted to make sure that no one who laid down his arms and surrendered would be shot. We knew that this would establish trust amongst the Palestinians (many of whom understood Hebrew) and might encourage them to surrender. Then we spoke in Arabic: "You have fought bravely and honorably. We can reach a peaceful solution to this situation. All men, aged fifteen to fifty-five, put down your guns and walk to Bassam's brick factory [a locally known site nearby]....The soldiers will not harm you..."

We repeated this a few times, but nothing happened. Nothing except prolonged minutes of silence in which nobody fired a shot. Suddenly it was dark. The term "twilight zone" well describes this transition from day to night, from known to unknown, from what feels safe to the darkness of uncertainty. Israel is located at a low latitude so that dusk falls quickly, unlike in northern latitudes, where twilight lasts much longer.

Due to the density of the buildings, we could not see what was happening in the next alleyway. We continued to call out again and again. I checked with the Shayetet teams positioned near the designated assembly place, but no Palestinians had shown up. Then we saw some movement. We instructed: "You! Continue to walk toward the soldiers. Put the guns down...keep walking." One by one, then in small groups, the gunmen started appearing. They approached the soldiers and were taken into custody. Those found to be uninvolved were later sent home. Over the next hour or so, 266 Palestinian gunmen surrendered. Our tactic had succeeded. Or so we thought.

Suddenly we heard shouts in Arabic. Then gunshots. Then all hell broke loose. Someone on the Palestinian side realized what was happening and wanted to put a halt to the surrender. A massive attack was aimed at our position. Heavy fire, hand grenades and IEDs exploded nearby. Helicopters fired cannons and shot missiles at the Palestinian outposts, hitting very close to our position. This friendly fire did not sound so friendly. The exchange lasted for several hours until, under heavy enemy fire, we were finally evacuated from Jenin and brought back to safety on the Israeli side of the line.

The fifty-five-mile *masa* from Tel Aviv to the Shayetet's base in Atlit

Captain Uri Teitz, the commanding officer of the Shayetet, shaking my hand on commencement day at the end of the twenty-month BUD/S training.
He tragically died a few weeks later.

IDF Chief of Staff Moshe Levy exposing my bat wings in the commencement ceremony

Commencement. I am standing at far right. Kneeling, third from left, is Yonat Dror, our team's admin.

Leading a forty with forty (forty kilometers carrying forty kilograms)
maximum operational scenario *masa* as chief instructor

The fifty-five-mile *masa*

As chief instructor, giving a final briefing before another *masa*

Brothers in arms – my team

Driving a high-speed cigar SEAL delivery boat, Atlit Bay

Zodiac Mark V rubber boat, during training

A high-speed cigar SEAL delivery boat, en route to distant enemy waters

Promoted to the rank of lieutenant commander, as the Shayetet's psychologist

As the Shayetet's psychologist, with Dr. Yair Schindel (*center*) and Tomer, an officer in the unit (*left*). This photo was taken in the midst of the annual Haifa–Akko seven-mile night swim.

Bay of Atlit; the Crusader castle and two cigars, celebrating Israel's Independence Day

An inspiring meeting with President Shimon Peres, with the first
cohort of Maoz, a network of leaders that we founded.
In the middle, next to me, is Dr. Yair Schindel.

At the FBI Headquarters in Washington, DC, talking about
"soft power" in counterterrorism

CHAPTER 15

The Psychic Toll of the Battlefield

Combat Stress Reaction

It was one hell of a night. My ears were ringing from the explosions, and I felt the adrenaline rush that characterizes the hyper-aroused physiological state induced by the battlefield. My heart was racing, my uniform drenched in my own sweat, and my perception of my surroundings seemed somehow altered. I was very focused and hypervigilant. My mind was busy thinking, rethinking, and to an extent, reexperiencing the battle. Vivid pictures of what I had seen, heard, and even smelled came back, again and again.

I somehow had to stretch and unlock the inner zone within my being and to start to reflect and begin what can be termed psychological damage control. I reminded myself that in extreme, life-threatening situations, our limbic system, an evolutionary part of our brain, activates the nervous system into what we recognize as survival mode, enabling the body and mind to prepare for a "fight or flight" or freeze reaction. Fight obviously serves survival. Sometimes running away is the right thing to do. Why freeze? Because in some situations you cannot run away and to fight back would be too dangerous, so the only option is to freeze and play dead.

In the Shayetet training course, the reactions to potentially critical situations are drummed into us. While practicing stealth movement at night, behind enemy lines, we were trained to freeze when an enemy patrol appeared and remain frozen until they moved on. You do not run for shelter or jump into a bush. You freeze. The reason that freezing enhances your chance of survival is biological and has evolved over millions of years. The same instincts allowed our ancient ancestors to avoid predators, to remain undetected, and to survive.

Combat stress reaction (CSR), I knew, could linger for hours or days and then dissipate to "normal." Normal is key because CSR is a normal reaction to an abnormal situation. When CSR does not go away, the same symptoms take on a new description: post-traumatic stress disorder (PTSD).

From the Battlefield to Everyday Life

At four o'clock in the morning, I found myself back in Israel, about five miles north of Jenin. My car was parked near Megiddo, the biblical site of Armageddon – yes, the same Armageddon that is mentioned in the Book of Revelations as the place where armies will gather at the end of days. For me, the battle was over, and I was outside the area of hostilities. I was back in Israel. But at that moment it felt as if I were in a totally different universe, a different reality. I got into my car and started the engine. It was time to go home.

American soldiers leaving Afghanistan or Iraq at the end of deployment have a long flight home. On the way home, the troops are given time to decompress and put their feelings and experiences into perspective. In a few days, they return to America and begin the long and sometimes complicated struggle to get back to regular service or to civilian life.

In Israel, this transition is much faster, perhaps too fast, because of the short distance from battlefield to home.

My family lives in a small village in the Lower Galilee, about a thirty-five-minute drive from Megiddo. I left the kibbutz in 1989. For the next nine years, Iris and I lived in a succession of rented apartments, until 1997, when we decided to make Alon Hagalil (Hebrew for "Oak of the Galilee") our home. The small community of Alon Hagalil is made up of farmers, high-tech entrepreneurs, engineers, people in health and helping professions, and others. One might describe it as the Israeli version of suburbia.

Driving in the direction of home on an empty road, I thought about the battle in Jenin that I had left behind only minutes before. Trying to comprehend and process this experience, I thought of Iris and the boys (at that time, our two sons), who undoubtedly were sleeping quietly at home, totally unaware of what I had just gone through.

How could I possibly share such an experience? What would I tell them? Would they be able to understand? These were the questions I mulled over during my short drive home. The boys were very young, and Iris is sensitive and understanding, but…sharing such experiences is a delicate matter. I had the feeling that it would be very difficult to describe the events in Jenin to someone who had not been there. It is extremely difficult to find the right words to convey the experiences and the accompanying feelings and sensations of the battlefield.

Many army veterans feel this and have a hard time sharing their experiences with their partners, friends, family members, and even with the therapists who are trying to help them. As a therapist and a combat soldier myself, it is, perhaps, easier for me to connect and enable this discourse with soldiers. I know the language; I have been there, and hopefully they have the confidence that I will understand.

But this time it was all about me.

My heart was racing, my mind spinning. I felt an emotional overflow. I asked myself, "How do I make the transition from battlefield to home?"

I drove up the hill and entered our village. It was still dark and very quiet. Even my fitness-conscious neighbors who enjoy an early morning run were still asleep. Our house was about a hundred yards downhill from a central parking lot. There was a narrow path leading to the house. I parked the car, lifted the heavy duffel bag containing the Kevlar bulletproof vest and helmet. I slung the rifle over my shoulder and started walking in the dark, toward home. The smell of gunpowder, my own sweat, and diesel fumes filled my nose. I needed a shower and maybe much more in order to unpack this tough experience.

On the sidewalk, just near the car, I noticed a familiar bicycle. It was one of those children's two-wheelers with training wheels. It was my son's bike. He had probably forgotten it there as he went off to play with friends. "I can't just leave it here," I remember thinking to myself, "someone might take it." I decided to take the bicycle, along with my heavy duffle bag, and carry it home. Negotiating my heavy load, I leaned over to pick up the bike by its handlebar. I found it extremely awkward holding on to the small bike in one hand while balancing my other cumbersome loads. I was bent over and felt discomfort in my lower back. "No, I can't do this," I thought. I felt as if my back were about to spasm, which might force me to be immobilized for the rest of this conflict.

On the battlefield, you don't just make big decisions. Under extreme stress, with the adrenaline rushing through your system along with the fight-flight-freeze reaction, there are many small decisions and thoughts: "Should I pass this house to the left or right? Maybe I should have brought that extra hand grenade with me, and oh…I'm tired and thirsty and my back hurts…"

I had to decide what to do with the bike. "Nah, I just can't leave it here…" But there was no way that I was going to walk that extra two hundred yards up and back just to get it. I was too tired and wanted to get home. Then suddenly, I heard my inner voice say: "Well, it's dark, there's no one around to see me…" In my army fatigues, duffle bag and rifle slung across my back, I hopped onto the little bicycle, lifted my legs, and allowed gravity to take me down the hill. As I stabilized myself with the accelerating speed, I felt a wide smile spread across my face and suddenly I knew: "Now I am ready to go home…"

Being able to smile, laugh, and let down my guard was what grounded me and pulled me back to normalcy. Gliding down the hill in freefall, I felt like an innocent child at play. Somehow it enabled me to put the traumatic, out-of-time recent events into perspective and to tie the disconnected loose ends of a shattered reality into rational terms.

These small "ceremonies" that soldiers perform when they return from a short mission, a violent patrol, or a long deployment are very important for the transition from the horrors of the battlefield back to normal, everyday life.

Casualties

The fighting continued in Jenin's refugee camp. Two days later, we went back in and were able to compel all of the remaining hard-core Hamas and Palestinian Islamic Jihadists to surrender. Operation Defensive Shield ended a few days later.

Most of the labs and workshops involved in the manufacture of suicide bomb vests were destroyed, and many terrorists were captured or killed. But it was common knowledge that many more terrorists were still out there. The conflict was (and still is) far from being over. During the following months, in the continuous struggle against Palestinian suicide bombers, the Shayetet operated on many fronts. The hunt for suicide bombers became a strategic mission whose goal was to bring normalcy back to the streets of Israel, to keep our children safe, and to enable Israel's thriving economy to bounce back. The only way to achieve this was – and still is – to continue to be on the offensive, to proactively search out the terrorists and arrest or hit them before they have the opportunity to attack.

During Operation Defensive Shield, a precedent was set for the Shayetet. Special forces seldom join large-scale tactical operations. In the past, they were called into action when their expertise was required to create a specific operational or strategic advantage. Because the arena of this conflict was situated in the alleyways of the Jenin refugee camp and in other Palestinian cities, it was imperative to avoid the collateral damage of harming innocent bystanders. The Shayetet was called in because of its abilities to manage this surgical mission in a tight theater of operation. Applying the Shayetet experience in stealth operations, it was felt, would keep unwanted casualties to a minimum. With the advantage of new technologies and intelligence capabilities, the Shayetet became the spearhead of the ongoing suicide-bomber manhunt.

The terrorists were always on the run, hiding in caves, in rural areas, and in apartments in Palestinian cities. The chase became more urgent as it was understood that the price for failing to find the terrorists on time would mean more suicide attacks in Israeli cities. Risks had to be taken to pursue them.

Until this point, we had been lucky during Operation Defensive Shield. The two Shayetet officers who had been wounded in the battle of Jenin, only hours after I had left, were treated and returned to active duty in the unit in a matter of weeks. We had a few near misses, but the unit was intact, and spirits remained high. A few weeks later, the situation changed, and we were licking our wounds.

Nir was killed in pursuit of a terrorist outside Jenin. His team was on patrol, combing an open, agricultural hillside. The terrorist they encountered was the first to open fire. Nir was hit and died instantly. During the years that followed, Avihu, Erez, Nathan, Roy, Moran, and Harel were killed in action. For a small unit, resembling a family, this was a hard blow to overcome.

On a personal level, my sense of loss was huge. Those were our finest men, some of whom I had trained and gotten to know well. On a professional level, the program for emergency intervention that I had initiated was ready to be activated. While conducting these interventions, I was a brother in arms, a clinical psychologist, and a grieving friend. It was challenging and gratifying to be there, trying to make a difference.

Integrating a Culture of Care

The term *resilience* is commonly defined as the ability to withstand a blow and to bounce back to normal functioning. Easier said than done. Returning to normalcy proved to be a great challenge for the leadership of the Shayetet. As the in-house consultant and part of the command team, I focused my work on the young team leaders. I introduced the concept of emotional debriefing and mentored the young lieutenants as they coped with the loss of close comrades. The idea was to help them internalize the concept that they must step into the role of "enabling parental figures" who were emotionally accepting as well as tactical combat leaders. It soon became apparent that strengthening their "soft" leadership skills also made them better combat leaders. With their new skills, they had a better sense of their men and were able to assess the atmosphere in the team. In this way, they would be able to intervene in the face of a traumatic event. This intervention might take place during a talk with the men in training, during debriefing, or even when going out for a beer together.

I remembered myself at their age and in their position, and I could relate to the way they were feeling and thinking as well as to their behavior. By bonding with them and gaining their trust, I was in a good position to help them lead their teams to cope with hard, potentially traumatic events.

Those were trying times. We struggled to operate and deliver operational results in the fight against suicide bombers. It was also a daunting challenge to deal with the loss of our finest men. I felt that I was in the right place to take professional action and design a program of intervention to ensure that the men were cared for and that the commanders were empowered to handle tough situations. The introduction of the "soft side of SOF" (special operation forces) proved effective in initiating changes in the operational culture of the unit: the stronger the bond between the men and their team leader, the better their operational capability. Out of loss and grief came a powerful sense of care. This caring leadership enhanced the unit's resiliency and operational capacity. In the following years, the Shayetet entered the fast trajectory lane, spearheading the IDF special forces and intelligence communities with innovative, creative, and out-of-the-box operations, some of which will remain under wraps for decades to come.

PART FOUR

A Time to Heal

The experience of working with traumatized individuals also brought back my own traumas, awakening old demons within myself. I was exposed, again and again, to their painful memories. This exposure has connected me with my own inner pain in a way that enabled me to start my own process of healing. Not only healing my patients, but also coming to terms with parts of my tortured self.

CHAPTER 16

From the Sword to the Plowshare

A Compass for Myself and Others

At the end of 2003, Daniel joined our family – a third son. Exactly three years later, Ziv was born, our fourth (and youngest) son. Four boys, full of energy and high spirits. Iris held down the fort at home, providing the means for them to grow and mature. For me, those were transformative years. I was immersed in my parental role, but I started feeling that it was time to move on professionally, and I began to contemplate my next career options. Being the Shayetet's psychologist, a therapist at the IDF Combat Stress Unit, and a hostage negotiator was very satisfying, but I started feeling an itch for change. I didn't have a clear idea what the next phase of my life might be, so I did what many seamen do – I stood and faced the wind, sensing its direction and strength; I gazed at the waves trying to detect the currents; I checked the charts for unseen obstacles that might compromise navigation.

I was trying to gauge what lay ahead for me, what opportunities were out there.

A weather vane and good seamanship are not enough. One needs to know in which direction to go. One needs a compass to show the way and help set the course.

When sailing, a skipper must divide his attention between the compass, the sea, the navigation charts, and the wind, as well as making sure all systems and the crew are functioning well. That is the logic that guided me as I was contemplating my next professional move.

As the Shayetet psychologist, I focused on what was happening inside the unit: recruitment, training, operational challenges, and dealing with situations of crisis and loss.

Soldiers came and went, sweated (and shivered) in training, graduated, fought, and were discharged after four and a half years of service. Later, I would meet them at the Shayetet base when they returned for reserve duty. Occasionally I received disturbing phone calls regarding a veteran who had veered off course and was not functioning well, either academically, in the workplace, or in his personal relationships. The calls came from parents, girl-friends, wives, or from other team members who had maintained close contact with their team members, even years after their service.

In most cases, I was not surprised to receive these calls. Knowing what the team had gone through and being acquainted with the minute details of the combat situations they had faced, I could never rule out PTSD. But unfortunately, it was not always diagnosed, let alone treated. In those cases, I tried to reach out, offer help, and refer the suffering ex-warriors to therapeutic resources in the community.

It was acknowledged that some Shayetet veterans had a hard time getting their lives on track. The transition from the adrenaline-driven service in the Shayetet to "dull" civilian life was a challenge. Some lost their way, doing drugs in exotic places around the world. Others were caught up in the "honey traps" of well-paying security jobs with no time to pursue academic degrees. Still others were just confused, unable to pull themselves together, and needed guidance to move forward with the next phase of their lives.

The transition from military service to civilian life is a major life change, and at the time, I did not fully understand the enormity of it. I was truly unaware of the significance of this transition. In retrospect, it seemed to me that that early morning bicycle ride downhill, following the battle of Jenin, became symbolic. At first it helped me recognize the challenge of coming back to base from the battlefield. Then it led me to recognize the challenge of homecoming. A few years later, the awareness of this process moved me to action, and I began to assist other soldiers in their transition toward the next phase of their civilian lives.

While reminiscing about my own experience of my first demobilization nearly twenty years earlier, I had a vivid memory. In August 1990, after five years of operational service in the Shayetet, I had decided to end my military term. At that time, I had no idea what I wanted to do with my life. One day, I just hung up my uniform, signed a few forms, and found myself on the outside, negotiating between my adrenaline-filled recent past and the blurry picture of my future. I began to feel anxious about my future prospects, and

I remember thinking, *Now what?* I sat at home in the small house Iris and I were renting, feeling out of focus. As I lay on the couch, I listened to radio reports from the Persian Gulf: Saddam Hussein had invaded Kuwait, and the world was heading toward the Gulf War.

I felt adrift. I began to search for a job, wondering what I was qualified to do and who would be interested in hiring me. It was a bitter realization, having served as a Navy SEAL, that this had little value in the outside world. I thought I had little to offer potential employers. It took great effort to formulate my next steps. I needed information and perhaps someone with whom to consult. In a pre-Google world, there were no quick answers, and I needed help to connect the dots and discover my evolving identity and in which direction to turn. In a sense, I was still struggling at this time with the effects of Dotan's mutilation and Ziv Levy's death. I was aware of the fact that I was struggling but wasn't aware that the source of this struggle might be post-traumatic stress. I needed time, support, and direction.

These thoughts and memories came to me during another time of personal transition. In 2008, I reached the end of my long military tenure and retired. This second transition to civilian life, when I was older and more experienced, proved to be almost equally challenging for me. Again, trying to tone down the adrenaline, the sense of purpose and worthy mission, I took time to consider what my next career move would be. As reality unfolded, I became immersed in the veterans' reintegration challenge. In the decade that followed, I founded and ran programs whose goal was to assist the transition of IDF veterans from service to civilian life.

Helping others reintegrate was my own way of moving from the sword to the plowshare, from being part of the military machine to caring for veterans. It undoubtedly helped me to grow and to heal my own invisible scars.

Creating the Reintegration Programs

Contrary to what many people may think, the main issue veterans face in their reintegration is rarely PTSD. Most often it's about moving from the battle of war to the battle of life. It's about crossing the bridge between military and civilian life. It's about figuring out how the years spent serving, training, and fighting can be relevant in finding and developing a successful career and future. The end game is about the veterans realizing their potential, putting their lives on track, and pursuing meaningful personal growth.

As Navy SEALs, these young combatants assumed enormous responsibilities. They integrated data and made life-and-death decisions on a daily basis. Their decision-making capabilities would determine the outcome of an operation, whether it would be a resounding success or a failure. They were trained to work fast, around the clock, under extremely stressful and uncertain conditions. They knew what it meant to take responsibility and to get the job done, applying the leadership training they had received. Soldiers also operate within the confines of a complex military organization. They learn to read between the lines in order to understand the intricate politics and how to navigate the formal, hierarchical establishment.

Fish might not be aware of the fact that they live in the ocean, but they must nevertheless know how to swim. Soldiers carry out their missions skillfully but are not necessarily aware of possessing unique knowledge and capabilities when they leave military life. Most of these young adults are just developing that inner voice of self-awareness. At this stage, it is important to bridge the gap between what they learned in the military and how to make it relevant and useful in their civilian lives. The challenge of reintegration is to help these young men translate and transfer the sense of competence and efficacy they had in the military to a sense of confidence that will support and guide them in their new lives. The other obstacle facing these newly demobilized men is the emotional challenge they face as they transition from military to civilian life. They need guidance and support.

Defining what successful guidance is all about, I recalled an experience I had as a young Navy SEAL. In late 1989, I took part in a submarine emergency exit drill in which a submarine, grounded at a depth of thirty to fifty yards and unable to surface, must be abandoned. The submariners must carry out a dangerous exit procedure. Beyond the complex technical issues, the submariner, once in the water, is catapulted toward the surface by the buoyancy of his life jacket. When you ascend rapidly, the external water pressure drops dramatically so that the air in your lungs expands, and there is the danger of barotrauma, a rupture of the lungs, which can be lethal. When you exit the sub and ascend to the surface, you do so without breathing. As opposed to the instinctive act of holding your breath, you are instructed to ascend, exhaling continuously to avoid rupturing your lungs.

We exercised this drill with professional divers inside a water tower thirty meters deep. After many prep sessions, it was my turn to carry out the sub-to-surface emergency exit drill. The instructor looked me in the eye and asked,

"Happy?" I nodded and he said, "Take a good, deep breath," and off I went. I started the long ascent, shooting upward, my mouth slightly open, exhaling like I was instructed. The tower is narrow, and soon I realized that I was not going up but was headed toward the wall at a dangerous angle. Instructors were posted along the way, free diving with goggles, following my movements. Each time I was about to bump into a wall, one of them would swim over, intercept my trajectory, and gently guide me back on track. It was those hardly noticeable correctional shifts that made a big difference. This type of gentle guidance and correction can change your trajectory and point you in the direction of your goal.

With this in mind, I crafted the post-military transition programs, which soon ran smoothly. I saw that the young SEAL veterans began feeling more confident and better equipped to move on. I also saw some positive results among some of the vets who had felt they were caught in limbo. They now felt as if they had a sense of direction and the momentum to make important decisions in order to go forward. Others who may have felt overwhelmed by the stress of everyday life now found the time and energy to look around and survey their options. Some started thinking about their own communities and of ways in which they could serve in a non-military capacity. As the programs continued to expand, we invited vets from other units to join us to learn and apply the model that was showing such success for SEAL veterans. A few years later, many similar programs were operating around the country.

Maoz: Empowering Veterans in Public Service

At the end of 2009, when the reintegration programs had been operational for a few years, I traveled to Boston. It was a fundraising trip, aimed to help scale up the programs. During the long hours at the airport and on the flight, I began to think about the reactions of some of the young Shayetet veterans who had participated in the reintegration program. They were showing an interest in the idea of giving back. They wanted to become involved in their own communities and to make a difference. This was the spark that initiated thoughts of going beyond the transition process. Maybe these same vets (and others) might be able to play on a bigger stage and effect real changes in their own communities and even in the country.

Arriving in Boston for the first time almost felt like a homecoming. The city immediately touched my heart. The New England foliage, the Charles River, and so much American history and culture – all of this touched me and rekindled memories of the "American boy" in me. I could still identify with the America I remembered and that had become part of my identity after a mere one-year-long stay in the Midwest, thirty-five years earlier. Walking across the bridge over the Charles River, through Back Bay and Beacon Hill, I was enchanted, not only by the Halloween holiday atmosphere, but by a deep sense of emotional connection. Familiar but long-dormant odors ignited lost memories, awakened parts of my being, and filled me with excitement and eagerness at the thought of spending more time in decoding the enchantment this city held for me.

On a cold November night during a dinner with good friends, we started to envision a new initiative. Dr. Yair Schindel served as the Shayetet physician when I was the unit's psychologist. After he completed his tenure in the Shayetet, having received one of the highest military awards for saving the lives of wounded soldiers during combat, he decided to change direction completely. He became involved in a startup for medical devices in Cambridge. While I was thinking linearly on the expansion of the reintegration programs and on incremental growth, Yair envisioned the creation of something much bigger: a game changer that would address the many challenges facing Israeli society, aiming to strengthen its public service institutions.

During an inspiring brainstorming session, we began to visualize the creation of a host of young leaders. The initial idea was to recruit special forces veterans, some of whom had already made headway in the high-tech startup scene and some of whom were now in corporate leadership positions. We wanted to empower them and encourage them to serve in local and central government positions and also in nongovernmental organizations. We hoped that they would promote change in the fields of education, welfare, and other underserved public areas. We were thinking big.

In a long process of experimentation, trial and error, we finally got the program up and running.

Maoz, the name eventually chosen for the program, means "stronghold" in Hebrew, a fortified center, a hub, and also forms the Hebrew acronym for leadership, values, and identity. The program gained recognition during the first years of its implementation and has grown to be an influential player in Israel, effecting change in both civil society and in public service.

CHAPTER 17

Across the Ocean

Back to Boston

With Maoz and the veterans' reintegration programs up and running, I found myself wrestling with the need to move on, to look for the next challenge. Again, I felt that it was time to make a change. In the summer of 2012, I relocated with my family for a year of study in Cambridge, Massachusetts.

Having made a commitment to promote social change upon completing my transition from military to civilian life, I felt that I needed more tools to advance my goals. I still had a few frontiers to breach. This opportunity to study was generously funded by the Wexner Foundation and was a part of the Wexner Israel Fellowship Program.

The mid-career master's degree in public administration is considered the flagship program of the Harvard Kennedy School of Government. Two hundred men and women from around the world take part in this academic program each year. They are all devoted to and passionate about public service. It was inspiring to be a part of this group. It seemed like an ongoing celebration.

There was so much going on around campus. There were lectures, parties, and talks by political and business leaders from around the world who came to engage and motivate us. As students, we felt as if we were at the epicenter of an amazing dream. Nevertheless, I felt that something was missing. I started having that strange yet not unfamiliar feeling, almost physical unrest, signaling a message to my inner self: Why am I only learning, talking, and dreaming, instead of doing something proactive? I felt the itch and the drive to do, to create, to be involved, and to be relevant. These thoughts slowly invaded my calm and disrupted my peaceful academic studies.

That was my mindset when I received a phone call from Dr. Jonathan Lewis.

Getting Involved with US Army Veterans

Dr. Jonathan Lewis is an inspiration and a close friend. We had met two years earlier in New York and had discussed the possibility of expanding one of the post-army programs. Jon expressed interest in becoming a partner. We met near Rockefeller Center early in the morning after he had completed his workout. He had spent most of the previous night in the operating room. Dr. Lewis is a world-renowned surgeon who has worked for many years at Memorial Sloan Kettering Cancer Center. With his heavy South African accent, his warmth and wisdom, he has an aura of magic about him.

After we shared some small talk and biographical details, our conversation shifted toward our parallel paths. We talked about fighting to save lives, about getting involved with the people we care for, and what it takes for a leader to serve and become a vehicle for change. We both felt that defining the way people and organizations think of and perceive the value of care and relationships is at the core of what leadership should represent.

About twenty minutes into the meeting, I paused and realized that fundraising, which was the pretext for our meeting, had not even been broached. It no longer seemed that this was the main reason for our meeting. This meeting became much more meaningful in ways that I did not fully appreciate at the time. Since then, Dr. Lewis has become a role model for me, as well as a cherished friend.

Jonathan was involved with the New York City Police Department (NYPD) peer support group, Police Organization Providing Peer Assistance (POPPA), an organization that assists policemen and women in the aftermath of traumatic events. This initiative started in the 1990s, at the height of the New York City crime surge. Cops were being threatened, shot at, and exposed to many horrific crime scenes. There was an increased number of suicides amongst policemen, many of these thought to be a result of constant traumatization. POPPA has succeeded in lowering the number of police suicides using a very powerful peer support model. Jonathan invited me to join him in his work, and I gladly came on board.

During the summer of 2012, the media reported on the skyrocketing number of suicides in the US military. The cover of *Time* magazine's July edition showed an American soldier holding a trumpet (at a funeral), and the headline read "One a Day." It was shocking to learn that every single day, an American serviceman or woman committed suicide. More American soldiers died by their own hand than by enemy fire. While this was troubling enough, further reading revealed that the suicide rate among veterans (there were about twenty million living vets at the time) was even higher. A vet committed suicide every eighty to ninety minutes, it was reported.

"The Pentagon is looking for ways to tackle this problem," Jonathan explained, and he asked me to present my work before the Task Force on the Prevention of Suicide by Members of the Armed Forces at the Defense Department in Washington, DC. In my presentation, I highlighted NYPD's model of peer support, which has proven to be successful in curbing suicide rates. I also spoke about the suicide prevention model used in the Israel Defense Forces, which has also shown encouraging results. The Israeli model focuses on training cadets in the officers' course – as well as training other junior noncommissioned officers – to identify soldiers in distress.

As I was speaking about suicide prevention in Washington, DC, I was reminded of the time, many years earlier, when I raised the possibility of initiating a similar program. In the months that followed, I assisted the US Ministry of Defense in the exploration of the various avenues of action for its suicide prevention task force. I was eager to help and attended working meetings and conference calls. During the time I was studying in the United States, this was my way of giving back and helping those who protect that great nation.

During my year at Harvard, I refrained from taking courses associated with psychological trauma, clinical psychology, or public health. I did not think that I would be going back to this type of work. Little did I know that in the not too distant future I would be dealing directly with psychological trauma during the aftermath of the Boston Marathon bombing.

Toward the end of the academic year, I started to consider my next career move. I had made connections in the fields of trauma and suicide prevention. I also became interested in the field of public administration and realized that I could make a significant impact in other ways. I was, however, not sure where my passion lay. Not yet.

The Boston Marathon

On the morning of April 15, 2013, I gave a lecture at Maimonides High School in Greater Boston. It was Patriots Day, and it also happened to be the Israel Defense Forces Memorial Day, according to the Hebrew calendar.

Every year, on Memorial Day, we would visit Iris's kibbutz to pay tribute to her brother, Ruvik, and to be with her parents. This was the first time we were not there.

I shared my personal story at the high school, highlighting Israeli reality to those Jewish boys and girls, depicting what "nation building" means and that we are still fighting for survival in the Middle East. When I pulled out of the parking lot after my presentation, I thought how removed these kids were from the experiences of Israeli kids, living under the constant threat of terror and war. I was wondering whether I had succeeded in conveying even a little of what it means to grow up in Israel, what it was like to hold a rifle and become a sniper at fifteen.

I didn't think that my experience was the default or the best way for children to grow up. It made me think about my own boys, who would soon be going back to Israel, growing up in this reality. Ori, my second son, was twelve at the time. He had accompanied me to the lecture and was impressed, hearing many parts of my story for the first time. I usually do not share my war stories at home. Despite living under constant threat, the kids in Israel today seem to have a more "normal" childhood than mine was.

On our way back to Cambridge, the GPS guided us into Boston's Back Bay area. Time and again I tried to turn northeast to avoid the traffic. But roads were blocked and many people, dressed in colorful outfits, were out in the streets. It was the day of the Boston Marathon. The weather was perfect, sunny and cool. I realized that we must be pretty close to the marathon's finish line on Boylston Street. Two of my classmates from Harvard, Nathan and Billy, both officers in the US military, were running in the marathon.

Finally, we managed to cross the Charles River and headed toward Cambridge. When we got home, we heard about the attack. Two improvised explosive devices (IEDs), built by the Tsarnaev brothers, were set to explode near the marathon's finish line. It was soon reported that the brothers were Chechen Muslims who had sought refuge in the United States and lived just a few blocks away from us. Three people were killed and hundreds wounded (many losing limbs) in the explosion. Boston was in a state of shock.

Over the next few days, the city was under lockdown. While the Boston police and the FBI were hunting down the perpetrators, all regular activity in the city came to a halt. Schools and universities were closed; people were ordered to stay in their homes. Boston, the hub of the American Revolution, one of the most peaceful and inspiring places in the world, was licking its wounds.

In Israel, most people have experienced wars, terror attacks, and surges of suicide bombings. This is not to say that we accept these as normal experiences. We have learned that such blows may throw you off your feet temporarily, but it is vital to maintain everyday functioning, to get back on your feet and return to normal as soon as possible.

Minutes after a terrorist attack, the Israeli media broadcasts a detailed picture of what has transpired, where the attack took place, and how many casualties were involved. They also provide the public with vital information such as emergency telephone numbers of hospitals and call centers to enable families to locate loved ones who may have been hurt. The actual scene of the attack is processed for forensic information and is immediately cleaned up and reopened to the public, usually in a matter of hours. Restaurants and other businesses hit by a suicide bomber usually open to the public in a matter of days. This is Israel's way to keep going. To be resilient.

Boston was different. Neither the public nor the government agencies had had to cope with a terrorist attack before. The local emergency systems, well prepared and highly professional, immediately went into action. Security teams appeared all over, their forces visible on the streets. Behind the scenes, enormous efforts were made to identify and capture the terrorists. But these measures took time and caused fear to spread. The disruptive effect of the terrorist attack, terror's goal, began to seep into the awareness of Boston's citizens. It was an attack on the safety of one's home and in a broader sense, it was an attack on the American way of life. The prolonged curfew with thousands of policemen in the streets was a huge burden for the Boston Police Department. Not only had they been unable to prevent the attack, they were exhausted and dispirited from working around the clock. Our support organization at the NYPD decided to reach out and help in any way we could.

A few days later, the NYPD team, peer supporters, and psychologists arrived in Boston. Over the next two weeks, we met, in various capacities, with the police units involved in the aftermath of the attack. I gave the opening talk, introduced myself, and shared my personal story. I told them I had served as a Navy SEAL officer and later as the unit's psychologist and had worked with soldiers who had experienced traumatic situations. My idea was to help them open up and loosen their inhibitions and psychological defenses.

I thought that sharing my experiences would engage them, thus encouraging these tough cops to share and work through their feelings regarding their experiences of recent events.

Next the NYPD team divided the policemen and women into groups of fifteen to twenty people for a more structured stress debriefing session. While they worked, I visited BPD stations to meet senior commanders, advising them on the importance of leadership and crisis management issues in order to reframe and put the recent traumatic events into perspective. In other words, to help them avoid, as far as possible, that invisible bullet of psychological trauma that can paralyze servicemen and citizens alike.

I was touched to see these brave men and women as they dealt with this terrorist attack. I saw the tears in the eyes of a bomb squad sergeant whose guilt at not being able to prevent the attack was visible; the exhaustion on the face of a senior commander who had been on his feet for four days and nights, unable to comprehend how such a thing could happen in his city; the anguish on the face of the policeman who stood guard for hours over the body of one of the victims. This scene of carnage would stay with him forever.

Close to seven hundred first responders met with our NYPD team. I continued to work with the BPD command for a few more weeks, meeting a large number of police service members. I felt that volunteering was a way for me to give back to the city which, I felt, had become my second home.

A year later, when I was back in Israel, Massachusetts governor Deval Patrick acknowledged the contribution of the NYPD peer support team and my own work with the Boston Police Department. In a ceremony at the Itzhak Rabin Memorial Center in Tel Aviv, leading Israeli organizations were honored for their contribution to the preparedness and assistance of the emergency forces that had been involved in the aftermath of the marathon attack. One of the organizations was NATAL – The Israel Trauma and Resilience Center.

CHAPTER 18

NATAL – The Israel Trauma and Resilience Center

Proactive Intervention for Trauma

While sitting in the therapist's armchair, I have assisted many soldiers and civilians in dealing with PTSD. Throughout the structured process, moments of horror, of a broken reality fragmented by painful memories and a sense of loss, were worked through. As a witness, I listened to the account of the dreadful events and assisted in the reconstruction of a new narrative. A narrative of healing. Caring for those soldiers was a most rewarding and transformative experience. But the experience of working with traumatized individuals also brought back my own traumas, awakening old demons within myself. I was exposed, again and again, to their painful memories. This exposure has connected me with my own inner pain in a way that enabled me to start my own process of healing. Not only healing my patients, but also coming to terms with parts of my tortured self.

It was rewarding, but it was so hard.

While trying to distance myself from this type of work by going away to study in Boston and exploring other career pathways, this experience has somehow led me back to working in the field of psychological trauma. I figured that those demons must have a place in my life, that I cannot really run away from them, and that if you can't beat 'em, join 'em!

This process of realization, of acknowledgement and awareness to psychological trauma, was also much needed on a national level, in Israel.

Jude Yovel Recanati founded NATAL in 1998. At the time, most victims of psychological trauma did not receive the treatment necessary for their recovery. Many were not even aware that they were suffering from trauma. The diagnosis of the invisible wound of trauma and therapeutic care were scarce. NATAL launched an emergency helpline and a small clinical unit which later evolved into a leading center for trauma, treating trauma victims, training clinicians, and raising the general awareness to the adverse effects of war and terror-related psychological trauma.

Jude and I had met years before, introduced by a mutual friend. She asked me to join NATAL, but at that time I was busy with my veterans' empowerment programs, so I told her that I was interested, but that it would have to wait.

In June 2013, having gained much experience working with BPD during the aftermath of the Boston Marathon bombing as well as through my involvement with NYPD and my participation in the Pentagon's suicide prevention task force, I felt that the time was right for me to join NATAL. Just before returning to Israel, I called Jude. "I'm on my way." I said.

The best way to treat psychological trauma is to prevent it. The concept of resilience as a shield to safeguard against trauma and the need to develop and sustain it has been at the forefront of psychological discourse for the last few decades. It has been a guiding principle for me for a long time.

While working with trainees in the Shayetet and relating to my own experience as a combat soldier, I could see the development of their professional and physical capabilities alongside the expansion of the mental skills required for coping with stress. They learned how to manage their own stress, to think clearly, and to make the right decisions in extreme situations. With this resilience, the well-being of the soldiers was enhanced when confronted with the dangers they faced every day.

During the Renaissance, Francis Bacon used the word *resilience*, derived from the Latin word *resilier*, to describe the ability to bounce back from a catastrophe, like an echo, a sound bouncing back off a wall. Later, the term was used in metallurgy and in the physics nomenclature in which resilience represents the amount of energy a substance can absorb without changing its basic traits. Today, in the social sciences, the term *resilience* is used to describe the internal flexibility necessary for a person or a community to be able to bend, not break, in the face of life-threatening (or other traumatic) situations. Even when a blow, a disaster, or a catastrophe is inescapable, resilience will guide you and help you get back on your feet.

At NATAL, I ran a team of therapists, counselors, and group facilitators. The team helped communities prepare for emergency situations, intervened in times of crisis, and helped victims of trauma recuperate following traumatic events.

On any given day, our routine of conducting resilience workshops and doing office chores was often interrupted by breaking news: "A rocket fired from Gaza hit a home in a town in southern Israel. Initial reports indicate that there are casualties. Emergency medical teams are operating on the scene." Or: "A suicide bomber exploded on a bus in Jerusalem during rush hour. Many passengers are believed to have been on and around the bus. We will update this story as more details become available."

As the media gathers more information and broadcasts a clearer picture of an unfolding event, I analyze the possible psychological repercussions and determine what interventions are necessary. During the hours and days following a crisis, psychological first aid is provided to those suffering from trauma and the grief of loss. Stress management procedures are conducted, and a proactive intervention plan is designed to assist the affected communities "the day after."

But psychological trauma has no boundaries and recognizes no ethnic or national affiliation. Israel's population is predominantly Jewish. There are, however, large minority groups, with the Arab society being the largest. In total, 21 percent of Israel's population are Arabs. Where I live, in the northern area, the Jewish and Arab communities are mixed, with the proportion being about 50:50. We also have large immigrant and ultra-Orthodox communities.

Working with all ethnic groups and denominations, my team consisted of professionals fluent in Hebrew, Arabic, Russian, English, French, and Amharic.

The Israeli Arab communities are especially prone to suffer psychological trauma. A hundred twenty years of Israeli-Arab conflict have left scars; being a traditional society that is transitioning into the modern Western way of life, losing some of its traditional checks and balances, and the sense of being caught in the middle of current hostilities have all negatively influenced this large community.

For me, working to support and heal, as well as to develop resilience among Arab communities, was of extreme importance. We have worked with individuals and families, in schools, welfare services, and local governments to enhance wellness and crisis preparedness.

Operation Protective Edge

The main scenario that kept me worried was full-scale war. When I took the position at NATAL, toward the end of 2013, I sensed that trouble was brewing. I recruited additional professionals and built capacity for large-scale emergency interventions.

In mid-June 2014, a few months into my new post at NATAL, three Israeli teenagers were kidnapped and held by Hamas somewhere in the Palestinian territories. Over the next three weeks, I was called to military service as a reservist in the Hostage and Crisis Negotiation Unit and was in close contact with Bat-Galim and Ofir Shaer, the parents of Gilad, one of the abducted boys. My role was to be there with the family, to update them with regard to the ongoing search for their son, and to prepare the family, should negotiations begin.

Confronting uncertainty is an extremely stressful situation. As the days passed and more data was collected, the chances of finding the boys alive dwindled. When the boys' bodies were found, it was the most unimaginable moment of grief. A few days before the news was received, I went with the family to the Western Wall in Jerusalem. The Western Wall of the Temple, destroyed two millennia ago, is the most sacred site of the Jewish people. Ofir prayed at the Wall for the life of his son. I stood near him, thinking how life's circumstances now connected me to this man and his family. When he completed his prayer, he turned to me and asked me to read a psalm. I took the Bible and started reading it aloud. It was the same psalm that we had read at my son Ori's bar mitzvah just a few months earlier. Ori was three years younger than the abducted boy. I couldn't stop thinking…it could have been my own son. It was an agonizing moment in which the boundaries between psychologist, reserve officer, and father became blurred. This situation is light years away from the secure setting of the therapist's clinic.

The abduction and murder of the boys marked the beginning of a very challenging summer. As Hamas increased its rocket fire, Israel found itself in another long round of violence. Operation Protective Edge, or as some called it, the 2014 Gaza War, had begun.

Working around the clock with individuals and communities all over Israel, my team provided help to those in need. This meant administering immediate psychological assistance to traumatized individuals, families, and communities. Many suffered the agony, disorientation, and pain related to loss, near-death experiences, and internal displacement. It was our job to reinforce the inner strength of individuals and communities to be able to cope with the situation. We hoped that in taking the initiative, we would be able to guide them to safety, to recovery, to resilience.

CHAPTER 19

Crisis and Post-Traumatic Growth

Disaster Relief around the World

While working in Israel I have, over the years, participated in disaster relief missions and emergency interventions around the world.

A geographically small country facing repeated rounds of violent conflict and terrorist attacks, Israel has confronted psychological trauma for decades. A vast body of research and expertise has been developed in Israel to enable communities and individuals to "bounce back" and function under duress. This knowledge, used by the experts to help trauma victims return to normalcy and to deal effectively with the aftermath of such events, has generated models of intervention that are used widely by the Israeli government and by nongovernmental organizations such as NATAL. They serve us well in dealing with emergency and disaster situations.

The relatively small Israeli community of trauma experts and mental health professionals working in various organizations has formed a unique ecosystem that enables the sharing of successful methods in order to act effectively in times of crisis.

Within this professional milieu, the Israeli Trauma Coalition, we seek to reach the same trauma victims and launch joint ventures. We cover each other's backs and help out when necessary. We have reached out to countries around the globe that have much less practical knowledge in crisis management than we do. We have shared our experience and expertise in trauma and resilience, helping others confront traumatic events as they unfold. Unlike Israel, which is in a constant state of alert, many countries are bewildered when facing the traumatic effects of war, a terrorist attack, or a natural disaster.

I had the privilege of working in the Philippines in 2014, training local educators and social workers in managing the post–Typhoon Yolanda crisis on the islands of Panay and Cebu. In this picturesque locale, seemingly one of the most peaceful places on earth, the language of active coping with stress, resilience, and crisis management was translated into the local Cebuano and Hiligaynon dialects.

The years 2016 and 2017 were rough ones in Europe. The Islamic State (ISIS/ISIL) carried out deadly attacks in Paris, Brussels, Berlin, Istanbul, London, and elsewhere. These acts of terror inspired lone-wolf attacks on innocent pedestrians using trucks and other vehicles as their weapons as well as random stabbing attacks.

Existing crisis management tools and procedures did not meet the urgent needs of the communities hit. Traumatized victims needed help, emotional first aid, and counseling. First responders worked hard and were exposed to horrific scenes of dead bodies, the moaning of the wounded, and the accompanying sense of helplessness and guilt for not being able to prevent the attacks. Municipal leaders had to mobilize their first responders to regain control and restore a sense of security. In the days following the attacks, they needed to lead their communities and generate resilience.

With the rising demand for our expertise, I shifted gear and began developing new training programs for better crisis management and leadership. I focused on tailoring the existing Israeli programs to fit the needs, as well as making the necessary cultural adaptations to suit major European cities.

Mass Shootings in the United States

While Europe was coping with this wave of terrorism, the United States, at this time, had relatively few radical Islamic jihad attacks. Obviously, someone was doing a good job of preventing attacks on US soil. But during my frequent work-related visits to the States, I could sense that something else was happening within American society. A series of mass shootings occurred all over America, taking the lives of hundreds.

The Orlando, Florida, nightclub shooting in June 2016, which left fifty-three dead and many more wounded, marked the beginning of this surge. In October 2017, fifty-eight people were killed by a lone shooter during an outdoor concert in Las Vegas. It seemed like a demon had been released, with so much violence that it was impossible to comprehend. There seemed to be no way to prevent these horrific acts.

In November 2017, a shooter killed twenty-six people in a church, near San Antonio, Texas. And it did not stop there. On the afternoon of February 14, 2018, Nikolas Cruz, a nineteen-year-old former student, opened fire at Marjory Stoneman Douglas High School in Parkland, Florida. Just before dismissal time, Cruz activated the fire alarm, causing students to open the classroom doors and to run into the hallways. With an AR-15 assault rifle, he shot indiscriminately. Seventeen students and staff members were murdered, and many others were severely wounded. Parkland, Coral Springs, and other neighboring communities whose teenagers attended this high school were in a state of shock and grief. So was America.

A little more than a week later, we landed in Miami. I was joined by Alan Cohen, a seasoned psychologist who had worked for decades with educational institutions and organizations, mainly in the north of Israel. We had a long flight in which to prepare our plans for this emergency intervention. We needed to know who our local partners would be, whom we would meet and assist, and who else was operating on the scene. Disaster relief attempts are like a dance: you want to make the right moves, join up with the right partners, and avoid stepping on other people's toes.

It was clear to me that the issue of gun control would, no doubt, arise and would be ever present. It was also clear that our work, aiding the survivors of this devastating attack, should be as detached as possible from the ideological and political chasm in America. We were representatives of the State of Israel; it was not our place to voice our opinions in this debate.

In a late-night briefing in the lobby of our hotel, the Israeli consul general asked me: "How will you reply when asked your opinion concerning gun control?" Thinking about it for a while, I had a vivid memory. I could not accurately date it, but it was probably from late 1973. It was a few weeks after the end of the Yom Kippur War, around my seventh birthday. My father was still in uniform, serving with his unit in the Golan Heights. We went to visit him in his army base on a cold Saturday morning. He took me for a ride in his military reconnaissance jeep. We drove east toward the armistice line between the Syrian army and the IDF. Here and there, burnt-out vehicles and tanks were still present, silent reminders of the heavy fighting. My father pointed toward the roadside. There was a barbed-wire fence with small yellow signs reading, "Landmines, beware." Minefields like this one were scattered over a large area near the Syrian frontier.

I reflected for a while, then said, "One of the first things that I learned as a soldier is that if you realize that you are about to enter a minefield, stop, don't enter." In this case, gun control and the Second Amendment debate were and still are a minefield. "This is an internal American issue."

The next morning, we went to work. First, we trained a small group of therapists working with the local Jewish Family Services, who became our partners. Then, we reached out to the community. Using social media, we got the word out that we were offering short, focused trauma workshops for parents, educators, therapists, and survivors.

Soon, we were inundated with requests for the trauma workshops. We were joined by other local mental healthcare organizations and became an integral part of the crisis management effort at the high school. We shared our crisis management protocols and our toolbox for dealing with "the day after" in schools and communities. We trained school social workers, mental health professionals, parents, and first responders. Survivors of the shooting reached out to us, and we conducted emergency interventions with them as well.

Timing was of the essence. During our stay, the teachers returned to school and started to prepare for the return of the students.

In Israel, air raid siren blasts alert the population of an imminent threat. When you hear the siren or the "code red" alert, you have only a few seconds to take shelter. Your heart is racing, you're sweating, and you feel panic set in. Then you hear the explosion and then more sirens – this time the blaring sirens of ambulances, fire engines, and police cars. Then it becomes quiet again. You slowly calm down and return to normal. But if attacks continue, trauma may develop. If it was a near miss or if people nearby were hit, it also affects you. Then, as in classical Pavlovian conditioning, the initial sound of the siren evokes an anxious reaction, even if it is a false alarm. The sound of a siren can reactivate traumatic memories and elicit panic and fear. Today, in Israel's bombarded southern cities and villages, this is a common reaction.

Upon entering Marjory Stoneman Douglas High School, passing dozens of media vans with satellite antennas, seeing the display of memorial signs, hundreds of teddy bears, flowers, and toys, I lifted my eyes and saw the fire alarm bell. It was clear to me that the next time the school held a fire drill, the memory of the alarm, activated by the shooter to draw out his prey, would reactivate traumatic responses. "There will be meltdowns, there will be panic attacks...," I thought to myself. It was imperative to convey our worry to the relevant authorities. Being made aware of this possible response, creating a supportive environment, and giving advance notice ahead of a drill would allow the principal or whoever activated the alarm the assurance that the students and teachers would be adequately prepared should a siren or fire alarm be activated.

It was an intense and meaningful mission. We felt the pain and grief along with the members of this community as they coped with the shock and disbelief that such a tragedy could occur here. We worked with those who were affected – students, parents, and emergency service workers. We felt their gratitude for our assistance, and they felt our empathy.

The Opportunity Embedded in Crisis

Working closely with traumatized individuals and communities, I have seen and felt the devastating pain they must cope with. When arriving on the scene, during what is often experienced as the darkest hour, I hold within me the understanding that many people and communities can actually grow and thrive out of the same traumatic experiences of war, terror, and loss.

Trying to negotiate my own confrontation with traumatic experiences as a child, as a young Navy SEAL and as an Israeli citizen, husband, and parent, living in this dangerous neighborhood, I find that what enables me to grow is giving meaning and purpose to what I do – the moral value–driven part of my day job and volunteer work.

When you do something worthwhile, when you give, you usually get something in return. We can learn something about this from a Hebrew word. The name Nathan, derived from the Hebrew word *natan* (spelled *nun*, *taf*, *nun*), means "he who gave." Interestingly, the word *natan* is a palindrome: it can be read from right to left and vice versa. The meaning of this can be that when you give, you also get back in return. Helping others (giving) and contributing your time, effort, experience, abilities, and resources makes you feel that you have a role to play. This can generate meaning and facilitate post-traumatic growth.

The term *crisis* is defined in English as "a time of intense difficulty, trouble, or danger." It is understood differently by other cultures. In Mandarin Chinese, the equivalent term is made up of two symbols or words: great danger and opportunity. In Hebrew, the term used for crisis is *mashbar*, derived from the word meaning broken, but in ancient Hebrew, it denoted the small stool used by a woman squatting in labor. Giving birth is a time of great pain and danger but also of an optimistic, happy beginning.

When I examine a crisis situation, I ask myself whether an opportunity is hiding behind or is embedded in the terrifying situation. Is there some new meaning or value that can be derived from the event that can lead to growth and a positive outcome? And of course, what can be done to help? How can I assist in making it happen? What value can I add to this journey?

CHAPTER 20

The Crises of Today and Tomorrow

COVID-19

An early memory: I am walking on the Mediterranean beach near the kibbutz. I am five or six years old. The sea is calm and beautiful. As I wander further away from my parents, I see something drifting in the water toward the shore: a big round metal ball, rusty, with metal horns sticking out of it. I had never seen anything like it before. Curious, I started out in the direction of this strange metal ball, walking toward it into the water.

"Stop! Don't touch that!" a loud voice yelled out from behind me. An adult kibbutznik rushed to me, blocking my path so that I was unable to reach the huge metal ball. He gently took hold of me, turned me around toward the beach, and made sure I continued to distance myself from the strange metal object.

"This is an old naval mine. It can blow up a ship. It's been at sea since the Second World War…but it could still explode if you touch it," he explained.

Things we experience in the present can often trigger buried memories. I had totally forgotten about that incident on the beach in the early '70s.

And all of a sudden the coronavirus burst onto the world stage, looking curiously like the mine that had washed ashore all those years ago. In the beginning of 2020, the novel coronavirus (COVID-19) started spreading like wildfire around the world. As more and more people got infected, nations took extreme measures in an attempt to contain the outbreak, enabling hospitals to cope with the influx of patients. On March 11, the World Health Organization declared COVID-19 a global pandemic.

The first time I saw an illustration of the coronavirus, I was thrown back to that memory of the naval mine floating toward the beach. What struck me was not only the similar appearance, but that they were both deadly. I thought

148

about the kibbutznik who warned me, distancing me from the danger. I also thought about how human interaction can spread the virus, reflecting on the role we as human beings play in situations of crisis – wars, pandemics, and other disasters. We create weapons and use them; we unknowingly spread infectious agents, but we also develop vaccines, care for others, and help them heal.

As nation after nation entered lockdown, it became evident that the COVID-19 pandemic, beyond causing severe illness and death, is sending shock waves through all aspects of our lives – cultural, social, and psychological. The impact on global economies has been devastating, with stock markets experiencing a freefall. Almost all economic activity worldwide came to a standstill during the initial lockdowns. There was fear and widespread panic in some regions.

As we learn to deal with COVID-19, our assumptions have changed, new strategies have been adapted, but still uncertainty prevails. Will there be a "day after"? Will social distancing remain? And for how long? Will we get our jobs back?

While isolating in our homes, we are all facing a new reality, unknown in our lifetime, which has aroused real fears. Fear of death, fear of sickness, fear for our older family members, fear of economic uncertainty. It is not an exaggeration to say that the coronavirus crisis has become a source of anxiety and trauma in our lives. The loss of a loved one, the near-death experience of a recovering patient, and the bleak economic future all have the potential to cause a magnitude of post-traumatic stress. Individuals, communities, and nations are being affected. PTSD is awaiting, just around the corner.

Given the unprecedented magnitude of the COVID-19 pandemic, I was afraid that millions of people around the world might suffer peri/post-corona PTSD and that traditional treatment protocols (psychiatric, psychotherapeutic) will be overwhelmed, too expensive, or unavailable to cover the enormous need and demand. I knew from experience that for many who might be wrestling with PTSD, there are other ways to help them bounce back to wellness and functioning.

During 2018 and 2019, I provided resilience training to police, EMS (paramedics and emergency medical personnel), and firefighters in New Jersey. It was a "train the trainer" program in which my trainees became trainers and brought resilience training into their agencies.

First responders are on the front lines of human suffering, and even before COVID-19, they were burning out and susceptible to various mental health issues.

As more and more people become infected by the novel coronavirus, hospital emergency rooms were overwhelmed, lacking the capacity to handle the overflow of patients. Medical teams, the real heroes of this crisis, started to show signs of burnout and fatigue. Afraid that they would pass the virus to their families, they wrestled with the conflict of going home versus staying longer hours in the hospitals; witnessing patients dying alone, without their families at their bedsides; and encountering unprecedented numbers of deaths. Many healthcare workers have been infected themselves.

I started getting calls from my former trainees. They shared with me just how bleak the situation was. With body bags on the streets in front of the hospitals, nurses and doctors in agony, hardly keeping up with the flow of patients, and the "moral injury" of having to decide which patient gets the ventilator and who will not, it all sounded very bad.

It became obvious very early on that help, in the form of resilience training, was needed to support the medical teams. But when exactly was there time for training? During the first weeks of the pandemic, I initiated a few interventions and provided support to medical teams in Israel and in the United States, focusing on the teams' functional continuity and enabling them to sustain their core mission of saving lives. But that wasn't enough. Something was desperately needed that could be scaled up for the many medical teams and first responders involved.

Exposure to a traumatic event can cause a break in the ties between the traumatized individual and his or her community. In the acute stress phase, following a traumatic experience, our ancient primal instincts drive us to seek shelter in the deep, dark cave of social (and many times physical) isolation. With the loss of social support, things can deteriorate fast. The isolation that was justifiably practiced with the coronavirus pandemic has the potential to accelerate this.

Real Talk to Fight the Epidemic of Loneliness

All this is happening against the larger picture of the ongoing loneliness and social isolation of today's technology-driven world. Even before the COVID-19 pandemic, many people were distancing themselves from others or felt lonely even in the company of others. In 2019, the World Health Organization declared loneliness an epidemic. It seems that while social media connects us in some ways, it is also creating distance between people. It discourages intimacy and disrupts bonding.

The more we text, use emoticons, and post well-staged and curated photos, videos, and text on social media, the less we talk and relate to each other. In the digital world, it has become harder to "real talk," to share actual existential experience. It has become harder for us to be on the receptive side of such real talk, to listen carefully without being judgmental, and to show and receive compassion.

Dr. Jonathan Lewis and I have been exploring ways to bring some of the ideas described in this book (caring leadership, resilience training, peer support) to larger organizations. We were joined by Sir Murray Brennan, a world-renowned cancer surgeon and Dr. Lewis's mentor and friend. Murray brought on board many years of experience and his deep wisdom. Nadav Cohen, a seasoned tech wizard and entrepreneur, joined our team just as we were starting to roll.

As the coronavirus pandemic surged, we decided to focus on peer support. Over the years, we have learned successful ways of enabling this with well worked-out, coordinated guidelines.

Our challenge was to do it all through the internet. In a matter of days, we built an app that can connect and facilitate real-talk peer support sessions via video.

Having worked for many years in the field of resilience, we have learned that this sincere face-to-face encounter is a major pillar that enables wellness and resilience.

The extraordinary power of mutual peer-to-peer support has been one of the major tools in our kit. In its basic approach, peer support reconnects us with our fellow human beings and humanity. It reconnects us with ourselves. Our sense was that in the midst and aftermath of the coronavirus crisis, our challenge is to relearn how to talk and share and how to listen without giving advice, without trying to "fix it." It is this exchange of human compassion that releases the stress, charges us with positive emotional energy, and enables the creation of a new and optimistic story in order to move forward and grow out of this crisis.

In Arabic, *dugri* means truthfulness, the opposite of a lie. In Hebrew, *dugri* (adopted from the Arabic) is slang for straight talk or real talk. Israelis are notoriously known to be straight talkers, blunt, *dugri*. We find it easier than people in some other cultures to share what's bothering us. To say it as it is.

Introducing *dugri* real talk to medical teams and first responders has shown good results. When many of us turned to video conferencing platforms such as Zoom to connect, study, or do business, I thought that this medium could be used to enhance resilience.

Dugri is a video-based peer-to-peer support and empowerment app that sets up and guides mutual peer support sessions. Dugri creates a safe space in which having each other's back and connecting at eye level serves as emotional PPE (personal protective equipment) for medical teams and first responders. Converting what has worked for us over the years into a digital platform, our goal is to create a new interpersonal sphere that strengthens resilience and lowers levels of PTSD. We believe that this is a highly effective way of bouncing back from the harsh emotional adversities of the coronavirus pandemic.

The Journey Continues

In the broader context of growing up on the kibbutz and serving the young, evolving State of Israel, I can look back at my service, as described in this book, with a sense of pride and accomplishment. What gives me personal gratification is seeing the programs and organizations I have been involved with continue to evolve after I have passed on the responsibilities to my successors.

My life has seen many crossroads. Again and again, I have felt the urge to move forward and change direction. I have felt the need to explore uncharted waters. It was necessary for me to develop and change on a personal level in order to be able to promote change in the lives of others.

Entrepreneurs tend to run fast, create new ventures, and build organizations from scratch. But founders of new ventures also need to know when to step aside, to move on and let someone else take the organization and the mission forward into the next phase.

Letting go is always a difficult personal challenge. In your head, you understand the need to move on, but your emotions may get in the way, interfering with the smooth transition from one CEO to the next. Some founders move to a position on the board of directors of their organizations, while others prefer to move on, knowing that their presence may cause friction and difficulties for the new management.

I moved on. While emotionally challenging, distancing myself allows something beautiful to happen: I gain perspective. I can see what I did not see while rooted deep within the venture. I watch the organization grow and change in ways far beyond my initial vision and strategic thoughts. Occasionally I visit the programs that I cofounded and take great pride in the role I played and where the program is headed now.

The after-army transition programs have grown and have been scaled to accommodate all IDF units. As an "open source" model, they were adopted, tailored, and recreated with additions that were introduced into their model. These programs have proven to be successful in empowering veterans of the Shayetet, other special forces, combat, and noncombat veterans in general.

Maoz network of leaders has been expanded, generating and inspiring new and innovative leadership programs and impact networks. It has started its own accelerator which promotes and boosts complex problem solving and has been recognized as a scalable model that has made a considerable contribution to strengthening public service in Israel.

In a wider context, Israel is climbing an uphill path, with a strong and growing economy, a unique innovation ecosystem, and an evolving youth-to-military-to-startup leadership pipeline of capable discharged soldiers who are creating Israel's and the world's future, today.

NATAL is deepening its crisis management abilities and is developing new ways of building resilience among individuals and communities.

The kibbutz movement has been struggling with the winds of change in a world that has moved swiftly from the "we" to the "I." The kibbutz has had to shift from a socially focused community to sustaining the community in an open-market world. The second-, third-, and fourth-generation members of my kibbutz have succeeded in keeping and harnessing some of the old values of commitment to the communal idea, mutual care, and responsibility and have managed to build Maagan Michael into a financially and socially strong and sustainable community. Maagan Michael has developed industries and advanced agricultural technologies into a global corporation, now publicly owned and traded on the stock market.

The Shayetet is constantly moving forward, shaping Israel's yet unwritten history, dealing with strategic and other urgent threats. No, I do not receive updates regarding current stealth operational work. I just watch the news and sometimes am able to read between the lines.

Over the years, mostly good memories of my military service remain. I still remember the cold water, the painful drills, the dangerous moments underwater. But I remember these as distant memories that elicit a grin now and not a grimace. The pain, the sense of loss, and the memory of our fallen remain our burden to carry. To carry on and remember. To honor their sacrifice.

Some painful memories remain, buried deep inside of me. Some of them occasionally pay me a visit. Moments of horror and near death, the moaning of the wounded, deafening explosions. I still relive traumatic events.

In late summer 2017, I received a phone call. It was Nilli, the community manager at Atalef – The Israeli Navy SEAL Foundation. Along with the veterans' program, they have initiated a new program aimed at assisting wounded Shayetet veterans. Nilli had an idea, something that I didn't have the guts to consider myself. "I had a long conversation with Dotan," she said. "He's come a long way in dealing with the loss of his leg. But he's still trying to piece together the events of that night. He's had some serious blackouts and has gaps in his memory of the event. He wants to know what happened."

Two weeks later, we met at the Shayetet base. Dotan arrived, walking on his one leg, using his crutches. Yaron and Ilan, who took care of Dotan in the ambulance, came as well. Just before the sunset, pouring beautiful colors over the calm sea, we walked through the entire event, putting the pieces of the puzzle together. It was not easy. It had happened nearly twenty-eight years earlier. Memories, especially hard and painful ones, tend to slip away and also to change, affected by other events and by other people's stories. Putting the pieces of the puzzle together, all four of us realized how limited was our personal recall of the event. By integrating our individual memories with an understanding of the facts on the ground (and underwater), we managed to form a coherent story of this horrible night.

Then we sat down around a small picnic table very near the exact spot where Dotan was hit and lay stunned and bleeding on that cold and stormy night in February 1990, when I ran to assist him and stopped the bleeding before the ambulance arrived. We talked and shared our memories and feelings, going back so many years, to one impossibly difficult moment. A moment that changed Dotan's life and our lives as well.

Dotan's rehabilitation was a long process. In dealing with his pain and loss, he turned to sports and has become a Paralympic athlete. He has won medals representing Israel in the games and has inspired many wounded warriors by sharing his story and offering encouragement.

Yaron became a healer. I remembered him as a tough and aggressive fighter, but after Dotan's mutilation and the loss of Ziv, the soldier who drowned that night, he changed. Applying Buddhist spirituality and Chinese medicine tools, he helps people.

Ilan, a down-to-earth, practical guy, took a different approach and left the whole experience behind. He barely remembered the event, which seemed to him a vague and distant nightmare. He became an accountant and works in finance. For him, emotional detachment has worked well over the years.

It was a very powerful and meaningful evening of closure. It was eye opening and puzzling at the same time to see how each one of us had been influenced by Dotan's mutilation and how, in the short and long run, it has affected our life trajectories.

As I have had to do during many phases of my career, I had to switch roles during this late debriefing session. Most of the time I was that young Shayetet team leader, wrestling with the loss, with the enormous personal and leadership challenge involved. At times I removed that hat and put on my clinical psychologist and trauma expert's hat, to reframe, to set the context, to lead this late but much-needed and effective therapeutic session. Looking back at my own journey, I can see how Dotan's blood mixed with my own emotional bleeding that night. I could see how this trauma led me to the course of personal development and to the professional trajectory of my life. Once again, the vivid notion of post-traumatic growth was evident.

Getting into my car, staring out the window one more time at the dark sea, I had an eerie physical-emotional experience of déjà vu. I could feel the salt water drying on my body. I could smell gunpowder mixed with the smell of blood. Loss and fear and the sense of urgency were present, as if it were happening at that moment, the explosion and the shouts echoing in the background of my memory. But this time was different. These reexperienced memories were accompanied by a sense of distance, perspective, and meaning.

Looking out the window, I felt that a few more demons, harsh memories of unfinished business, could now be released. In my mind's eye, I saw an ageless figure holding a long trident, walking back into the sea. It had been a long journey across the boundaries of pain, trauma, and destiny to the gratifying feeling of relief and closure.

I had a deep feeling of a mission accomplished. We had come a long way.

I believe all four of us slept soundly that night.

Acknowledgments

During the long process of writing and publishing this book, I have been supported and encouraged by many. Uncovering lost memories, weaving them into my personal and professional journey, and articulating the ideas and insights that stem from them was challenging and somewhat disconcerting at times. I was and still am very fortunate to be surrounded by people who inspire me and reach out to help, including friends, colleagues, and family.

I wish to express my deep gratitude to Nigel Risner for giving me the first push to start. A special thanks to Nancy Ayalon for her in-depth linguistic and content editing of the initial draft and for providing me with her profound perspective on parts of my story which were hers as well. Nancy's guidance, support, and hard work took this book to a totally different level. In the process of publishing this book, I have found a new home at Gefen Publishing House. I wish to express my warm feelings and gratitude to Gefen's team, especially to Ilan Greenfield for believing in me; to Kezia Raffel Pride, for her magic touch in editing the final draft, and to Daphne Abrahams for connecting all the dots and getting the book to print.

I am grateful for the wise comments of Reuven Gal, Itamar Eder, Sagi Melamed, David Lonner, Ronen Koehler, and Ophir Falk regarding the flow of the book. I greatly appreciate Dr. Jonathan Lewis for his encouragement and for connecting so many threads in my life. I am very grateful for my friends and mentors Jeff and Debbie Swartz and Jonathan and Faryl Sandler for being my Greater Boston family and hub. My sons, Neta, Ori, Daniel, and Ziv, could have benefited from the long hours invested in writing this book, but nevertheless encouraged me to write it. As every sailor knows, setting sail, going out to the high seas is only possible when one has a safe haven to return to. Words cannot express the love and support that Iris, my wife and partner, managed to grant me. For all of these, I am so grateful.